Why does no one talk about knowledge in this school?

A conversation between Grace Jackson, Angela Oakley and Henry Welwyn, heads of science, English and history at the Riverside Academy, East London.

Recorded and edited by Henry Welwyn.

I

Henry Welwyn: I have a question for you guys. Why does no one talk about knowledge in this school?

Grace Jackson: What do you mean? We talk about knowledge all the time. We're currently having lots of conversations as a department around where to place disciplinary knowledge in our curriculum. We have our knowledge organisers; we talk about how to chunk new knowledge to avoid too much cognitive load; our CPD sessions are based on developing pedagogical content knowledge. How can you say we don't talk about knowledge?

HW: OK, so I grant that we use the word 'knowledge' in conversation, but what are we actually talking about when we use that word?

GJ: It's what helps us understand the world. It's the stuff we must pass on to our students so they are not ignorant when they leave us.

Angela Oakley: Can you give an example?

1

GJ: Well, in science, we want students to know lots of things. Biology tells them what they need to know about their bodies to stay healthy. Chemistry explains how substances react and change; they can't understand loads of everyday things without knowing that. Physics explains how everything moves and interacts, how anything electrical works, how energy moves around, and so on. They couldn't understand most of the world around them without physics.

AO: Couldn't they? I never really understood anything in science, but I seem to cope just fine in the world.

GJ: But you would cope better if you did understand. Knowing how to wire a three pin plug means you can change a fuse if it blows in your kettle. Knowing what concentration means makes you more likely to put the right amount of screen wash in your car so the water doesn't freeze on a cold day.

AO: But I don't need to know these things! If my kettle broke, I'd just call an electrician. And I just follow the instructions on the back of the bottle of screen wash; I don't need to know why I'm adding a certain amount.

GJ: So are you saying the knowledge we give to students is pointless?

AO: I'm not saying it's pointless. I'm sure it's useful for someone, somewhere. What I would argue is that we get way too excited about knowledge and miss what I think education is really all about.

GJ: What's that?

AO: For me, it's about self-discovery. It's about emancipating yourself from the norms society places upon you and learning how to think and act freely. Too often, at school, we focus on filling students' heads full of facts. We forget that they are living human beings, who have a right to learn how to think for themselves.

HW: How do you think we should support them to do this?

AO: Well, when I read a text with my students in English, I'm not really interested in telling them about what such and such an episode is a reference to or what technique the writer was applying on page 79. What I'm trying to do is give them a window into their own soul. For me, it's by reading about and reflecting upon the experiences of others that we can truly come to understand ourselves.

GJ: But surely there's knowledge involved in this? You need definitions of words, first and foremost. There's no way you can understand what a text is talking about unless you know what the words mean.

AO: Of course, but my point is that you have to start with the meaning of the whole text and only afterwards focus on the individual words. Students have to be engaged before they start learning definitions. Otherwise you kill their motivation and they don't want to read the text at all.

GJ: I'm not sure about this. I would argue that if students know what the words mean then they're way more likely to enjoy the text. If they're trying to read something they don't understand then the cognitive load is surely going to be way too high. They'll be putting all their energy into decoding and will have no capacity to make sense of the broader meaning.

AO: So what, you think we should make students memorise the dictionary first before we allow them to read any texts?

GJ: No, of course not. That would be crazy. All I'm saying is that you can't understand Shakespeare unless you already have a broad vocabulary. We need to explicitly teach students the meanings of words before we introduce them to the most important texts.

AO: Well, that's another thing: why do we have to teach students Shakespeare? Who says his plays are the most important texts?

GJ: Surely we can all agree that any study of English literature should involve the study of Shakespeare?

AO: Perhaps, at some point. But why do we have to start with Shakespeare? That's the problem we have in this school, we just do what we've always done. In English we have to teach Shakespeare, in history we have to teach about the Tudors, in science we have to teach about the famous discoveries of all those dead, white men. None of this stuff speaks to students; it has no tangible impact on their lives.

HW: What do you think our role as educators is?

AO: To liberate our students, to enlighten them, to empower them. We have to let them know that the world is not fixed, that power structures are open to change, that history is still being written. Yet all we ever seem to do is the opposite. In science, you guys tell them, "here are a load of facts about the world, you just need to remember them." In history, you go on and on about the past without ever telling them how this might relate to their lives in the present. And now you're telling me that in English we should stop talking about their own lives and instead tell them a load of stuff about Shakespeare. It's too much!

HW: You don't think Shakespeare has relevance to their lives? I always thought he was addressing some pretty universal themes.

AO: Well, that's arguable, whether you can take the perspective of a white, European, educated male from the early 17th Century as universal, but I'll grant it to you for the sake of the argument. All I'm saying is that we have to consider our students' starting points. They are growing up in a world that is very different to the one Shakespeare lived in. If you go to his texts too early, you switch them off entirely. They need to be motivated to find out more about themselves before being introduced to those traditional texts.

GJ: I'm sorry, Angela, but I think you're just plain wrong here. Firstly, this whole thing about students being motivated before they can learn anything is nonsense. It's by learning things that they *become* motivated. My students enjoy learning science because I teach them how to do things and then give them an opportunity to practise. Once they get the hang of it and feel that success, they feel good. It's that feeling that motivates them to learn more. I just don't buy all this lighting fires bullshit, I'm sorry.

AO: But what does success even mean? You're dictating -

GJ: Hang on, hang on - let me finish. Secondly, I really don't think you can claim that the themes Shakespeare is talking about are not universal. It doesn't matter who you are, where you come from, what era or society you were born into: you are going to experience feelings of ambition, of love, of jealousy, of pride, of despair. Shakespeare addressed those themes better than anyone before or since, and there's no way we can help students understand themselves in the way you're talking about unless they know a whole lot of stuff about his plays.

Finally, even if those themes weren't universal, if what you say about Shakespeare's perspective being limited to a certain time or place is correct - well, those plays still happen to be the plays that people in power have read and can talk about, so we 100% owe it to our students to give them a decent working knowledge of those plays in order that they can take part in those conversations. Because if we're saying, "oh, those kids in that private school might learn about Shakespeare but our kids in this school are going to learn about something more 'relevant'," we're denying them access to the very power structures you're saying you wish to overcome.

AO: But isn't that just the classic liberal position! First, you set the rules of the game so that they entirely suit your preferences. The students who accept those rules 'feel that success', as you described it; they are the ones who are indeed motivated to work harder. The students who don't accept those rules, however - students who, I might add, tend to be from working class or minority backgrounds - are branded as 'low ability' and end up being spat out of the system as failures. And that's after they've endured years of punitive behaviour systems forcing them to play a game that bears zero relation to the lives they actually lead. The system is rigged and you know it.

GJ: But how is anyone ever going to change the system unless they're part of it? That's what I'm saying! The only way we can change the system is if the kinds of students you're talking about have the opportunity to become part of it. What you're suggesting ultimately just preserves the status quo.

AO: I know that's what you're saying: you're saying that we have to take the power structure for granted and hope that by forcing working class and minority kids to be compliant then they won't get screwed over quite so badly. What I'm saying is that we need to question the whole structure. We need to liberate our minds from the way we've always done things and think about how we could redesign the system altogether.

II

HW: I'm interested in the point you made about behaviour systems. Do you think our school is too strict?

AO: I don't think there's anything wrong with being strict. My mum was super strict, and I'm grateful to her for it. But I think that as teachers we occupy a very different position to that of parents. We are representatives of the state, and I think it's problematic when a state-funded organisation, staffed mostly by white teachers, is going into a diverse area like this one and punishing students for failing to adhere to rules imposed by people who do not represent the community.

GJ: Are you saying we shouldn't have rules, then?

AO: That's not what I'm saying, no. What I'm saying is that we are representatives of a democratic state and that we must therefore make sure we have democratic processes in place to decide on the rules we must all adhere to.

GJ: Such as?

AO: Such as ensuring students have a voice within the school. Such as maintaining close links with parents and never forgetting that the role of the school is to serve our community. Maybe even such as teachers co-constructing the rules of their classroom together with their students so that everyone is bought in.

GJ: So you're against centralised behaviour systems?

AO: My concern with centralised behaviour systems is that they represent a kind of faceless, bureaucratic power. There are teachers in this school who use this behaviour system in a way that benefits themselves rather than the students. They hide behind the system because they haven't put the work into building those relationships. What this leads to is students not respecting them: they obey through fear of punishment, not because they think they should. You end up with a sort of doublethink, where students say what they need to say to stay out of trouble, but don't really believe in it. And if this is the case, then have we really educated those students? Have we changed who they are as people or have we just changed the way they behave within that building?

Then there are the ones who refuse to conform. They refuse to accept the rules and end up being excluded from class, then from school, and ultimately from society. And, like we said before, who are those students who are most likely to end up getting excluded? It's those 'low ability' ones again, the ones who happen to be predominantly from working class and minority backgrounds.

GJ: But I've seen you teaching, Angela. You're one of the strictest teachers in the school! And I've definitely seen you exclude students from your classes because they've been disrupting your lesson. I don't see how you can argue against that.

AO: I can be strict because my students respect me. They also know how deeply I care for them. I am from this community: I know what it is like to grow up here; I know the challenges they're facing; I also know what it's like to bring up children here, given I've got two of my own. That stuff matters.

GJ: Which is all well and good, but does this mean we should only recruit teachers who grew up in the same community as the school? That doesn't seem feasible, or indeed desirable. I'm not from this community, and I think I do a pretty decent job of teaching science. So, assuming we can't and don't wish to do that, what hope does a new teacher, fresh out of university, have if they're going to teach at a school that doesn't have a centralised behaviour system? It takes years to earn the kind of respect you've accrued; do they just have to suffer while they wait for it to build up? If so, well, they're probably going to get sick of teaching altogether and leave the profession, or maybe they'll go and find a nice, cushy job in an international school where the students actually respect them. Isn't the kind of thinking you're advocating a major part of why we have a retention crisis?

AO: The reason we have a retention crisis is because of ever-increasing accountability coupled with ever-decreasing autonomy! Teachers are constantly being told what to do and how to do it, and if they dare to have an opinion of their own - to, shock horror, act as thinking, reflective professionals - then they live in constant fear of being thrown off the bus altogether. I'm lucky in that sense: because I have been around the block a bit and get results, I know they're unlikely to just get rid of me, but even then I'm still having to argue constantly with SLT about how I should do my job. It's a nightmare. If I didn't love the kids so much, I'd have left a long time ago. Maybe they'd be happy if I did leave; they could just put on one of those online video lessons and get the kids working in silence that way.

HW: It's interesting, Angela, that you've essentially made the same point three times: once regarding knowledge, the fact that students who don't accept the need to learn Shakespeare are branded as low ability; once regarding behaviour, the fact that students who refuse to play by the rules end up getting excluded; and now regarding teacher autonomy, the fact that teachers who want to adopt their own methods are likely to be forced out. Do you think the same thing is going on in each case?

AO: I think so, yes. I think in the last ten or fifteen years education has been taken over by a small group of people with a very clear ideological agenda - I'm thinking Michael Gove, Michael Wilshaw, those sorts of people - an agenda that's tied up in the whole academies and free schools movement, in the changes to the National Curriculum, in the way we're being asked to teach now and how that's all bound up in the new Ofsted inspection framework. And I think that whole agenda is based on a very narrow idea of what it means to live a good life. Basically, those people believe that everyone should be reading Dickens or Jane Austen -

GJ: Or Shakespeare.

AO: Exactly! Or Shakespeare, and they effectively think that if you don't read those sorts of books, and if you don't have an encyclopaedic knowledge of the Battle of Hastings and the Magna Carta, and if you don't have this deep love of biology or chemistry or physics, well, in that case, you must be somehow deficient. Likewise, if you don't come from a culture based on sitting and discussing the news at the dinner table, if you don't hold yourself in a certain way when walking around the school, if you're expressive and passionate rather than being all English and *restrained*, then you're labelled as some sort of miscreant and sent to the isolation room. And if you're a teacher who doesn't believe in all that cognitive science, retrieval practice, direct instruction nonsense; if you believe that teaching is about passion and enthusiasm and love; if you're more interested in building relationships between you and the students than having arguments about whether they're allowed to have their coat on or not, then you run the risk of being told that you don't know how to teach and being placed onto a support plan. And it's all in service of this ideal of Britishness - 'British values', that old chestnut! - this middle class, middle aged, typically male idea of what we should do, how we should behave, who we should be. Grace, you're shaking your head. You don't agree with me.

GJ: I mean, I kind of see your point, but I can't get on board with a lot of what you're saying. We've talked about Shakespeare already and I don't want to go over that again, but I really don't see how you can argue that teaching young people about science is some sort of middle class indoctrination.

AO: But do we teach them about science, or do we just ask them to memorise a bucket load of scientific facts that they don't really understand? That's certainly my memory of being taught science, although I appreciate that was a while ago.

GJ: The two aren't mutually exclusive! It's not an either/or between understanding and facts: the understanding comes *through* learning the facts. There's a body of evidence showing how we need a broad base of knowledge to be stored in our long term memory in order to solve more complex problems or carry out more complex tasks. And that's not just true in science, that's true in English too. That's why knowledge organisers are so powerful: they help students commit the core knowledge into long term memory so that when it comes to solving a problem, or writing an essay, or interpreting a newspaper report, or whatever, students' working memories are not overloaded.

AO: You know my thoughts on all that working memory, long term memory stuff, Grace …

GJ: I know all too well, Angela, but again I just don't get how you can argue that applying the verifiable findings of cognitive science is part of some middle class crusade against society. Surely it's just good teaching?

AO: Is it? Let's take knowledge organisers as an example. I saw one made by someone in my department recently. It had the definition of the word 'hubris' on: 'excessive pride'. Students were able to parrot the fact that hubris means excessive pride, but when I asked them to give me an example of hubris, they looked at me like I was from Mars! This is what I'm saying: teaching English is about more than teaching knowledge.

III

HW: We're coming back to my original question. Is the problem knowledge, per se, or is it that what we're calling 'knowledge' is somehow deficient, something that falls short of genuine knowledge? That's what I'm interested in: what does it mean to know something?

GJ: You two: classic humanities graduates, always trying to make things more complicated than they need to be. We all know what it means to know something. If you can remember it, say it, do it; well, then you know it.

HW: I'm not sure it is so simple, though, Grace. I was observing one of your team teaching chemistry to Year 9 recently. The lesson was about calculating the number of moles in a gas.

AO: Goodness me, I feel queasy already.

HW: Bear with me, Angela! So the point is that this teacher was teaching the students really well. She brought in all the I do-we do-you do, checking for understanding, deliberate practice, and so on. She modelled the first example, showing them how to identify the right numbers from the question using the units; she then showed them how to substitute the numbers into the formula; finally she did the calculation and showed them how to write the answer down with the correct units. After she'd done the first example, the students did another example on their mini-whiteboards. She checked everyone's work, gave some feedback, then gave them a few more examples to complete independently.

GJ: I'm happy to hear that everything we've been practising as a department is actually happening in lessons.

HW: It is, for sure, and it's really great. It feels pacy, punchy, slick; there's an energy in the room, students feeling that success that you mentioned earlier. But there's a problem.

AO: What, that it sounds like an Orwellian nightmare?

HW: Well, that, obviously, but a serious problem too.

GJ: Go on.

HW: Once the teacher had set the students off on the independent task, I circulated the room a bit, as she was doing too. You could see students doing the questions and she was ticking their work, which suggested they knew what they were doing. I went up to one student, after the teacher had given him a tick, and asked him about what he'd just done. I think it was a question on HCl - does that sound right?

GJ: Yes, I can imagine that being one of the examples.

HW: OK, so let's say it was HCl. Now, I'm not a scientist, so I'm not an expert on these things, but I seem to remember H being hydrogen and Cl being chlorine?

GJ: It certainly is: house point for you, Mr Welwyn.

HW: Thank you, thank you. So I asked this student, knowing only a very small amount about what he was doing, what HCl meant. I asked him what it was and what it looked like; he just looked at me blankly and shrugged his shoulders. I probed him a bit further and he said to me, "I'm not gonna lie sir, I'm really bad at science. I'm just good at maths."

GJ: Typical.

HW: I dare say it is, and that's the interesting point. This student could do the question, he could decode all the words, I'm sure he could identify the correct units and so on, but he actually had no idea what he was calculating. I could have replaced the words in the equation he was using with nonsense words - red equals blue over green or something - and he could have followed exactly the same procedure and churned out exactly the same number.

GJ: Well, no, because, as you said, he has to work out the number for each quantity from the units.

HW: But the teacher could have told him, red has the units 'moles', blue has the units 'grams', or whatever. He could have committed that to his long term memory and been perfectly capable of solving the problem. He knows something, clearly. But what does he know? I'm not sure it had much to do with science.

AO: Exactly! These methods train students to be mindless automatons; they completely miss the point of education.

HW: I'm not sure I'd go that far. I happen to think there *is* a role for these techniques. In fact, I thought the way she taught the lesson was brilliant. The problem was not with the methods, it was with what she was using the methods to achieve.

GJ: What do you mean?

HW: I think the problem was that the teacher was focused entirely on the outcome, rather than the thinking required to achieve that outcome. She very effectively gave them a tool to solve that problem, but the students were left without any appreciation of what the problem actually was in the first place. It might as well have been a game or a puzzle: the students simply had to learn the rules and apply them to achieve the desired outcome. There wasn't much sense that what they were doing linked to anything out there in the world.

AO: But that's exactly my point. These methods are very good for training students to memorise facts and procedures, but those facts and procedures bear no relation to the students' actual lives.

HW: I think that's a valid critique. We have the same problem in history. We spend a lot of time modelling how to answer 9 mark questions on the exam paper, giving students various rubrics and techniques to help them score full marks, but what this leads to is students thinking about how to score 9 marks on the exam question, rather than thinking historically, about their own lives or otherwise.

GJ: I think you're both trying to get to the end point too quickly. Of course, at some point in their lives we want students to be able to think for themselves, to apply their knowledge to new and unusual situations, to relate what they learn to their own lives and the world around them, but surely we can't start from this point, otherwise we're presupposing students have already reached the state we're trying to get them to. The kinds of things you're talking about are complex tasks made up of a large number of component procedures. It's only through extended practice of these procedures, so that each one is forged into a student's long term memory, that the student is able to synthesise them into a fluent performance. That's what we mean by mastery. I won't bore you both with football or baseball analogies but it's the same principle.

AO: Those analogies are misleading, anyway. A student who likes football doesn't mind practising procedures, e.g. doing passing drills, because they have a sense of how this component fits into a broader whole. Whereas what you're advocating is never giving students a glimpse of the whole until they've practised all the procedures and achieved this so-called 'mastery'. Unless we give students a glimpse of the whole early on, there's no way they'll ever be motivated to put the practice in that's required.

HW: I think you make a very good point, Angela. I'm thinking about it in terms of a journey.

GJ: Oh God, this sounds corny. *'It's not about the destination; it's about the journey.'*

HW: Bear with me! Let's imagine I want to go from my house in Leyton to Oxford Circus in Central London. Maybe I want to go shopping or something. The quickest way for me to get there is to take the tube. I can jump on the Central Line at Leyton station and emerge exactly where I want to be. This is all well and good, but besides my start point and end point I have no idea where I've been. Now, let's say the thing I was looking for is out of stock at the shop near Oxford Circus, but the person in the shop tells me they have availability at their store in Piccadilly Circus. If my only knowledge of where I am is based on the tube map, then I'm going to have to go all the way back to Holborn on the Central Line then take the Piccadilly Line three stops down to Piccadilly Circus. But if I actually know my way around central London then I can just walk down Regent Street and be there in half the time.

GJ: How does this relate to teaching?

HW: My point is that we want our students to know their way around our disciplines. We want them to be able to think fluently and intuitively without having to rely purely on the methods we give them. What I saw in the science lesson I described earlier was equivalent to putting the student on the tube at Leyton station. He emerged with the right answer, but he had no idea where he'd gone to get there, or even where he was when he started. It's almost as if the method was *too* efficient, *too* effective at getting him to the destination. By tunnelling the student straight to the correct answer, the teacher actually prevented him from thinking about what he really needed to think about.

GJ: OK, I see your point. I've always hated formula triangles but never really known why. I think this is a helpful way of thinking about it.

HW: Exactly. So there are two issues with what I saw in that lesson. The first was pointed out by Angela: the students were practising but with no idea about why such practice was important, to what broader whole this task related to. This is a bit like the students being told they have to go to Oxford Circus without being given any reason why. And when it comes to our disciplines - solving science problems, writing history essays, reading poetry - many of our students have no idea why anyone would want to do these things in the first place.

The second was the nature of the task the students were being asked to practise. I take your point, Grace, that students really do need to practise component procedures before they can carry out a broader, more complex performance, but as teachers we need to choose the correct procedures to practise. What I saw in the science lesson was a lot of students being sent to Oxford Circus and back on the tube. What they needed to be thinking about was the underlying *concept*.

GJ: What was the underlying concept?

HW: Again, I'm not a scientist so I'm not 100% sure, but I guess it had something to do with the idea of the mole.

GJ: That's definitely something students find difficult.

HW: I can imagine, and that's why it's essential that we get students thinking about it. The same can be said for other important concepts. It's only by asking them to think in terms of these concepts that we can give students a feel for the broader disciplinary landscape. Every task that prompts them to think in terms of a new concept is an opportunity to practise walking individual sections of the journey above ground. It's not just about getting from A to B: it's about knowing how A and B sit in relation to one another as well as to all the other ideas of the discipline.

This kind of approach is inevitably going to take a lot longer, but I think it addresses Angela's objection about making student learning more meaningful, while still taking into account your arguments around developing mastery and fluency.

IV

GJ: What you've said is interesting, especially the second point, around what we're asking students to think about. Willingham talks about this in detail.

AO: Willingham! Don't talk to me about him.

GJ: Why not? Surely you don't disagree with his findings?

AO: I just think all those people - Willingham, Kirschner, Rosenshine, whoever - they all miss the point. They all take teaching as some sort of transmission process, and learning as memorisation. It's all about filling students' heads with facts. It's just such an impoverished version of what education is all about.

GJ: But it's not! You're attacking a straw man. Willingham is explicit about how memories build around narratives and schemas. We have to tell stories to our students, to sequence the content we cover in order that these schemas can develop. It's not just 'memorise this'. He's saying we have to build that knowledge by constantly making connections back to what students already know.

AO: I know, I know, and you're going to show me one of those little spider web diagrams now aren't you, lots of little dots and lines all joined together in a perfect pattern. It's nonsense! It falls so far short of what makes our job meaningful.

HW: What should education be about, Angela?

AO: I've said it already: it's about transformation. Every lesson should turn our students' worlds upside down. They should come out of it a new person. I want to constantly give them new experiences, disrupt how they operate in the world, challenge them to think differently. So much of what we do in this school does the opposite: it forces them to look backwards, reinforces habits and common sense, forbids them from having any new ideas of their own. It's always the end of the conversation, rather than the beginning.

GJ: But they can't take part in any conversation unless they know stuff! Good luck trying to talk to someone about science if they don't know what atoms are. There is stuff in the world that you just need to know, and surely it's our job to pass that on? Maybe it's different in English, I don't know.

AO: I think it is different. As I said earlier, we don't teach students texts so they have a good knowledge of the text; we teach students texts so they have a window into themselves. English as a subject is not about what you have by the end of it; it's what you do with afterwards that matters.

HW: I think Angela's conversation metaphor is useful here. I would argue that teaching is always the end and the beginning of the conversation at the same time.

AO: What do you mean?

HW: I mean that Grace is right insofar as our disciplines have produced knowledge that can now be codified into the kind of information you might write down in a knowledge organiser or refer to in a retrieval quiz. You can write down that atoms are made up of protons, neutrons and electrons and pretty much take that as a given, at least for the purposes of schooling. But by taking it as a given, you must be aware that you're putting a stop to the process; you're calling it the end of the conversation whether you realise it or not. And Angela's right to say that the knowledge we pass on to students must retain a certain degree of openness. They must always be able to *do* something with it in the future. It must always be the start of a conversation as well.

GJ: I don't agree that teaching students facts makes it the end of the conversation. You teach students that stuff so they can use it and apply it later on. Of course no one wants to just end the story; it's just that the deeper level of understanding we're all aiming for can only arise once you have a solid base of prior knowledge.

HW: I think I'm making a slightly different point. What I'm trying to say is that the fact that atoms are made up of protons, neutrons and electrons is not something 'out there' in the world, ready to be taken and placed into a student's head. It's the outcome of a certain disciplinary process. That's the conversation that ends when we tell students a fact, the process of generating knowledge.

GJ: I don't understand. Atoms really are made up of protons, neutrons and electrons. There's a whole body of evidence to support this.

HW: But that's the point. How do we know this fact? Well, because some scientists -

GJ: Thomson, Rutherford, Chadwick -

HW: Yes, those guys - they went through this whole process, the purpose of which was to show others that what they were claiming was true.

AO: But is it even true? I seem to remember being told that everything we got taught about atoms in school was actually wrong!

GJ: It's not wrong, it just gets a bit more complicated once you start to study it in more depth.

HW: Exactly, and it gets more complicated because you get deeper into the historical process. That's what we need to -

GJ: Hang on, hang on - so you agree with me that atoms being made up of protons, neutrons and electrons is a fact.

HW: Yes.

GJ: And you're saying that this fact is only a fact because of the work that was done by scientists like Thomson, Rutherford and Chadwick.

HW: Yes.

GJ: So what's your point? Just because scientists did some work on it doesn't change the fact that it's a fact.

AO: "The fact that it's a fact." Such a science teacher!

GJ: No, but seriously. I don't see what you're arguing for. Honestly, I don't really care who came up with these ideas. What matters is that they're true, and for that reason I owe it to my students to pass them on.

HW: But we can only say these things are true *because* of the historical process. The Bible tells us the Earth is 6,000 years old, and this was taken as true for a long time because it was written in the Bible. We now don't believe in this number, because there was a whole process of gathering, sharing and discussing new evidence that implied the age of the Earth was much greater.

GJ: Fine, so all this stuff is covered in our spec. We have this key ideas section about how scientists use models and interpret data and so on, and we teach them a few bits about the history of science: the development of atomic models, the history of the periodic table, evolution, all that stuff. They're not my favourite parts of the course but we definitely cover them.

HW: I suppose what I would argue is that you can't just 'cover them' and move on. The ideas of science can only have meaning to students if they have a sense of how they were generated in the first place. It's the same in history. I could tell them about how this happened, then this happened, then this happened -

AO: That's how I was taught history. It was awful!

HW: Well, me too, but for some reason I carried on with it and started to enjoy it a bit more later on. My point was that when I teach my students, I want to give them a sense not only of what happened or what it was like in the past, but how we can find out what happened or what it was like in the past.

GJ: How do you do that?

HW: Well, one example is a unit we do on a historian called Emma Griffin. She wanted to find out what life was like for women during the Industrial Revolution, but the problem was there was very little direct evidence available. People didn't really write about what life was like for women, and women certainly didn't write autobiographies or anything like that. So she had to piece together clues from the autobiographies of men, from newspaper reports, and so on.

GJ: Oh God, source work! I used to hate that when I was at school. I think it's why I dropped history; it was so boring.

HW: I can sympathise with you there, although I wouldn't say what I'm talking about is quite the same as old-fashioned source work. I mean, I still want students to go away knowing some facts about what life was like for women in the early 19th Century. I guess I'm arguing that it is only through teaching the facts that the process of being a historian can be made clear. And it's in that sense that facts are both the end and the beginning of the conversation.

AO: I don't like the way you're talking about this stuff as a process. It's not like this Emma Griffiths person -

HW: Griffin.

AO: Sorry, Griffin - it's not like she was thinking, "OK, first I'm going to do this, then this, then this," and at the end of it, "there you go - here's some historical knowledge!" I'd bet a lot of money that she was feeling her way by intuition: late nights at the library; days and weeks of despondency interspersed with moments of inspiration; hours spent looking at stuff that led nowhere then suddenly finding a goldmine. We try to package these people's work up as if they were following simple, codifiable processes but that's just not what it's like. What matters is that she had that desire, that passion, that desperate need to find out more. Surely it's that fire which we need to ignite in our students?

GJ: There you go, Angela, lighting fires again.

AO: But it's true! You just want to fill students up then send them out to have boring conversations about stuff no one cares about. I want to make them human beings: passionate, inquisitive, alive.

GJ: Not true! I want to make them interesting. I'm interested in talking to people who know stuff, who can think interesting thoughts and tell me things I hadn't heard about before. I'm not particularly interested in talking to someone who has a passionate desire to shoot their mouth off yet doesn't know the difference between Darwin and Dickens. I'm interested in speaking to people who are educated.

AO: And there you go again: if you don't know about dead, white, European men from the 19th Century then you're not educated. It's like talking to Michael Gove!

V

HW: I think we're starting to get to the heart of the matter here. What does it mean to be educated?

AO: Big question!

HW: It is a big question, but I think we have to be clear on how to answer it before we can do anything else.

GJ: Really? I disagree. I see a lot of teachers spending hours chatting about this stuff but then I walk past their lessons and the students aren't even listening anyway. In my department we're focusing on doing the basics right and will worry about this abstract stuff once that's sorted. That means microscripting routines to ensure we have consistency across every classroom; instructional coaching to give teachers actionable feedback that can make their teaching better immediately; and responsive CPD targeting the things we think are slipping.

AO: That sounds horrendous! I'd go crazy if I taught in your department! Don't you want to give your teachers any autonomy whatsoever? Don't you think it might be a good thing if they can think for themselves?

GJ: But they don't need autonomy over everything. I don't need autonomy over everything. I don't really care what routine I use for getting students into the classroom, or cold calling, or checking for understanding using whiteboards. I just want to do something that works and that is consistent across the school. Autonomy over this stuff frees me up to spend more time thinking about how I'm going to explain a certain idea, what misconceptions I need to tease out when I check for understanding, what makes for good deliberate practice.

AO: But you don't give your staff autonomy over that stuff, either. You guys use booklets, don't you?

GJ: We do, but it doesn't mean teachers can't make changes or suggest better tasks. It just means they always have a starting point. This seems a lot less stressful than having to plan every lesson from scratch, every time.

AO: I don't know. To me, teaching is an artform. I want to express myself in the classroom, and I think that's what my students really relate to, that's what inspires them. I don't think you can reduce what I do to techniques or 'microscripts'. Just saying that word makes me shudder!

GJ: Aren't you just being self-indulgent though? As much as I'd love to express myself, what's more important to me is that my students leave school with the knowledge they need to lead good lives and participate in society. Maybe if we worked in a private school then I could teach the periodic table through a haiku or Henry could teach the battle of the Somme through interpretative dance, but here in East London the stakes are just a little bit too high. If we mess it up, these kids are screwed - we all know that - so I'm going to go with what the evidence tells me are the best bets for helping them learn.

AO: But this is just so reductive. You're probably a phonics advocate as well, aren't you?

GJ: I'm not an 'advocate', Angela, I just know there is a strong body of evidence supporting the fact that phonics works.

AO: Works for what? Helping students 'decode'? Practising 'phonemes'? We're back to where we were before: my point is that you're never going to *want* to read if your only experience of reading is through phonics. We don't break down texts into tiny little fragments: we take in whole words, sentences, paragraphs, and we relate the meaning of those to the way we live our own lives. You want to make reading a meaningless activity, learning a meaningless exercise, and teaching a meaningless profession. I'm sorry, Grace, but it makes me really sad.

GJ: Don't worry, Angela, I've known you long enough not to take it personally. All I'm saying is that my main focus is on every student making as much progress as possible during the limited time we have them at school.

HW: What interests me is the parallel Angela has picked up between your approach to learning and your approach to teaching, and indeed between those and the phonics approach to reading. It seems as though what you guys really disagree on is whether to start with the parts or the whole. Grace, you're saying we should start with the parts: decoding individual phonemes before reading whole sentences; mastery of basic techniques before moving on to more complex tasks; microscripts and actionable step feedback before conversations about curriculum intent and the broader aims of education. Angela is saying we have to start with the whole: getting the meaning of the sentence first and only then going into the nuts and bolts of the words; getting stuck into more challenging tasks as a route into the more granular detail; understanding teaching as an expression of the whole person rather than as an aggregation of techniques.

What's funny is that this seems to be a reflection of your subjects. Science is all about breaking a problem down into the smallest possible components and building up from there. That's what Descartes was talking about in his Discourse on the Method. Whereas literature is all about capturing the unity of experience, about seeing how everything is related and ultimately inseparable.

GJ: You mean, science deals with reality whereas literature is just made up.

AO: Grace! If you were one of my students I'd be making a phone call home right now.

GJ: I'm sorry, Angela, I said that just to wind you up.

AO: It's actually a fair point, though. This is the impression a lot of students have when they come to my class. I have to explain to them that the themes we address in our texts are just as real as anything they cover in their other subjects.

GJ: But you're dealing with feelings and emotions, right? And I'm asking that as a serious question, not just to troll you. My point is that we're dealing with objective reality whereas you're dealing with subjective reality. They're both important, just different.

HW: I think Angela might contest your claim.

AO: I most certainly would! I always get very wary when people start talking about 'objective reality'. Scientists like to claim they are the only ones with the right to discuss this so-called objective world but they're human beings too! As Henry pointed out earlier, they're having to make subjective judgements about things all the time. They have to carry out their experiments and interpret the evidence. You can't just ignore that. This is how science ended up in a situation where I got taught a lot of stuff about atoms when I was at school, only for my teacher to tell me that, actually, none of it was really true. Atoms don't look like those little spinny things we see in the pictures. So who am I supposed to believe?

GJ: But you do believe that atoms are real, don't you?

AO: Kind of, although to me, the emotions Romeo and Juliet go through are a lot more real than atoms. Why can't we call those 'objective' instead?

GJ: Glad to see you used an example from Shakespeare there.

AO: Only for your benefit. Have you heard of Romeo and Juliet? I know you scientists find reading difficult sometimes.

HW: Now then, you two, now then. I'm not sure I agree with either of you on this. I think there is something to be said for the subjective-objective split, but I don't think it's as clear cut as Grace suggested. I think all of our disciplines are aiming at a sort of objective reality: this is just as true in literature as it is in physics. The point of the disciplines is that they're trying to capture and make sense of experience. So when Wordsworth climbs Snowdon at the end of the Prelude and sees the mind of man in the mountains and misty valleys, what he's experiencing then is as real to him as the electrons a scientist sees when conducting some experiment in quantum physics, or as Napoleon's thought process is in the mind of the historian as she pieces together everything that happened in the lead up to him crossing the Niemen.

GJ: 'The mind of man in the mountains'? What?! He didn't see any mind; he saw mountains. Anything else was just a projection of his own internal states onto the external reality surrounding him.

AO: You do not have a poetic bone in your body, Grace! You can explain it away all you like in terms of projection or wish fulfilment or some other psychological term, but that doesn't capture what it *feels* like to be a poet. I'm with Henry on this.

HW: Well, I think you might go too far, Angela, and bury any sense of objectivity underneath that feeling. Grace may *feel* she's made a great discovery in physics; I may *feel* I've uncovered some brand new insight into Napoleon's march towards Moscow, but that doesn't entail knowledge. The reason Wordsworth's feeling has endured is because, after reading him, lots of other people have gone up Snowdon and experienced something similar. We can only call that experience 'objective' if it goes beyond an individual person, if it's felt more widely by a whole community or network of people.

GJ: But can we call it objective? Maybe it's worth me repeating: there is not a mind hanging out at the top of Snowdon. There are just some other mountains. That's the reality.

HW: But this is where we have to understand how the different disciplines operate. Science, at least pre-quantum physics, is based on the assumption that there is an external reality that we can make sense of through observation and measurement. Poetry, at least the Romantic poetry that I'm talking about, is based on the opposite assumption, that there is no 'external' reality, no boundary between inner and outer states. If you're starting from that position, in which all experience is unified, then the weather, the landscape, the expressions on the faces of the people around you, even simple objects in your kitchen, all have a meaning. They are just as much a part of your being as your heart, your nervous system, your eyes. And if enough people agree that this is the best way to make sense of reality, then the meanings they generate move beyond the 'subjective' experience of one slightly eccentric person, and become a shared, 'objective' reality.

GJ: But they're not real! Just because lots of people think they're real, doesn't mean they are. Take the Earth being 6,000 years old. Literally everyone in the Christian world thought that was reality, but it wasn't. It's just a fact that it's not the case.

AO: So what, are you telling me love isn't real, or pride, or guilt, or envy? Because the last time I checked, literature has a lot more to say about those things than any scientist can.

GJ: Well, to take the first example, love, it's an evolutionary thing, right? We fall in love and form family units as a survival mechanism. It's just natural selection.

AO: You're getting married soon, aren't you, Grace?

GJ: Yes, in the summer.

AO: Are you going to walk down the aisle and say to your husband, "I promise to always do what's best for the survival of the species"? No! You're going to give him your whole person and merge your life with his. That's what love is. Science has nothing to do with it.

HW: It's a good example, and I think it illustrates my point. You can look at love from many different angles: from a religious point of view, from a poetic point of view, from a scientific point of view, from a sociological point of view. The point is that we really do fall in love; that's something that definitely happens. Each discipline is an attempt to find a means of explaining it. And I think Angela's right to say that science tends to make out that it's got a monopoly of truth when it comes to making these explanations, whereas I agree with her that there are many aspects of human experience that are explained as or even more effectively by other disciplines.

VI

GJ: I'm interested in what you've been saying, although it's definitely not how I would usually think about things. Give me some examples of stuff that's better explained by other disciplines.

HW: To come back to what we were originally talking about, I think knowledge is a pretty good one.

GJ: Why's that?

HW: Well, let's start with how science - cognitive science - understands knowledge. Remember that science assumes the external world exists and that the way we can make sense of it is through observation and measurement. So if we're going to understand knowledge, cognitive scientists argue, then there must be something real and material that exists and that we can measure. Hence they say things like, 'learning is best understood as a change in long term memory'. They say this because, supposedly, we can measure memory in an objective way.

GJ: Why 'supposedly'?

HW: Because to make the measurements objective, they typically have to ask participants in their trials to remember and retrieve nonsense words and phrases.

AO: Why?

HW: It's to make the test fair. They can't control what the people taking part in their trials know or already know. If they were asking people to remember words or phrases linked to basketball, and one person happened to know loads about basketball, you wouldn't know whether that person remembered stuff because of what the researchers were changing or because they knew a lot about it anyway.

GJ: That's just good science.

HW: It may be good science, but it's problematic when it comes to understanding what goes on in the classroom, as opposed to the research lab.

GJ: Why?

HW: Because we're absolutely not in the business of teaching students nonsense words and phrases. We want what students learn to be meaningful; we can't ignore the knowledge and understandings they bring with them to the classroom.

AO: This is exactly what I was saying! Retrieval practice is very good at getting students to memorise words and phrases, but half the time those words and phrases are meaningless to them. Think about those students telling me hubris means excessive pride. Those might as well have been nonsense words for all they understood of them!

GJ: But the problem here isn't with cognitive science. The problem here is how cognitive science is applied to classroom practice. I agree that there are an awful lot of lethal mutations, but these happen because people haven't read the science properly, not because the science is wrong.

HW: This is a fair point. I think the problem is that many people - including certain members of our SLT - treat cognitive science with a certain deference simply because it's science. As we were just discussing, science has this air of objectivity which makes people think it must be able to explain everything. But I think we're a long way from getting a robust scientific theory of knowledge. I'm not sure such a thing could even exist in the first place.

GJ: What about Rosenshine? What about Willingham and Kirschner? Haven't they given us some useful pointers?

HW: Well that's it, they may have given us some pointers, but when they do that they're straying out of the realm of science and into the realm of practical advice. I think we have to be clear about the difference between theory and practice. Theory is descriptive or explanatory. It doesn't take a position on anything; it simply aims to state how things work. So when Kirschner talks about working memory vs long term memory or Willingham talks about building schemas, they're trying to explain what's happening when we think and when we remember stuff. These are both interesting projects. Good luck to them.

The problems arise when they start saying things like, "working memory is easily overloaded, so you should do x in the classroom." As soon as you start throwing 'should' statements into the mix, you're presupposing the aims and ends of education, and that's not a debate that science can say anything about.

GJ: You sound like an academic, Henry, wittering on about the aims of education. We already know what we want to achieve. We want our students to get the best grades possible so they can live better lives. If you don't agree with that, then I don't think you should be working in this school.

AO: Stop! You're just unbearable sometimes! Of course I want my students to achieve good grades, but I also want them to enjoy the time they spend with me before they get them. I want them to take away something more than just a bit of paper. Does that make me a bad teacher?

GJ: Of course not - I also want my lessons to be enjoyable and I want students to love learning my subject, but aren't we all agreed that the aim that trumps all others is for our students to leave with strong outcomes?

HW: I think there are two things to be said here. One, that you're betraying your scientific mentality again, Grace, in that you're desperate for everything to be measurable. We're back to our question about what it means to be educated: can we measure everything that makes for a good education or are there aspects of it we will never be able to capture?

AO: I would say that none of the good stuff can be captured, but you probably knew that already!

HW: The second thing I wanted to say is that exam results aren't actually an aim of education; they're more a way of ascertaining whether or not the aims have been met.

GJ: What do you mean?

HW: Well, as I just said, any assessment is a form of measurement, but, to use your language, what's the variable here?

GJ: Whether they know stuff or not, and I suppose whether they understand it or not too.

HW: Precisely, but that means we have made a decision somewhere along the line that it is a Good Thing for students to know and understand stuff. Exams are just a means of measuring the extent to which we've achieved our aims. The problem is that knowing is intangible and difficult to describe. What we measure and how we measure it always has to be dependent on the conception of knowledge we're aiming for.

GJ: So what do you think we're aiming for?

HW: This is where it gets messy. There are multiple aims present in every classroom, and unpicking them is difficult. I think there are two spectrums we have to consider: the spectrum of individual aims through to societal aims, and the spectrum of general aims through to specialised aims.

GJ: This sounds complicated. I might need to pop to the loo.

HW: Stick with me! I'll try to keep it brief. Basically, one way of looking at the aims of education is in terms of the student: how does education make their life better? In general terms, it gives them a broad introduction to the ways humans have sought to make sense of the world, which helps them balance all the competing desires and interests they have in their own lives. The idea is that, through education, they may live with a sort of inner harmony, in which they know a little bit about everything rather than loads about one thing and not much about anything else. A more specialised education would be one that allows them to develop some of their desires and interests more fully than others and pursue them to a much higher level of proficiency. From the individual's point of view, this means doing more of what you love and less of what you don't love. It also allows you to make more money. But there is a danger that you lose this inner harmony and end up ignorant about important aspects of what it means to be a human. This is a tension that we have to deal with.

A similar tension exists from the point of view of society. The question here is: how does education make society better? In general terms, we educate students so that they can be good citizens and take part in the democratic process. We want people to have shared meanings and reference points so they can get along better and not find each other strange or threatening; likewise, we want people to know enough science, history, and literature that they will make informed political decisions and not elect populists or dictators. But for society to innovate and make progress, education must also be specialised. It must give people the opportunity to challenge established ideas and come up with new ones. The danger with an overly specialised education is that society fragments, and everyone becomes so wrapped up in their own way of thinking that the shared meanings and perspectives get lost. Consequently, we descend into a sort of intellectual anarchy. Again, this is a tension we have to deal with.

VII

GJ: You say we have to deal with this tension between general and specialised education, and take into account the individual's aims vs society's aims. My question to you is: *do* we have to deal with this stuff? Or are we just teachers? I feel as though these sorts of questions are of interest to academics and politicians but not really relevant to those of us who are actually working in the classroom day to day.

HW: I think it's helpful to be clear on these issues for two reasons. Firstly, so that we can begin to understand one another better and hopefully engage in fewer arguments. I think the main reason you and Angela fall out is because you find it difficult to relate to each other's implicit aims.

AO: It's not that - it's because she's so bossy and acts like she knows everything!

GJ: I can't help it, Angela: I'm a scientist.

HW: But you see what I mean? I would say Angela's aims are much more focused on the individual than yours, Grace. She wants students to be emancipated from society's strictures, whereas you want the opposite, that they become part of society. Likewise, you want education to be much more specialised - split into subjects, lots of rigorously selected knowledge, teacher as the expert - whereas Angela wants to keep things quite general: less emphasis on subjects, a focus on the whole of human experience, teachers and students engaged in more democratic relationships.

GJ: OK, so it may help me to understand Angela better, but how is this stuff going to help me in the classroom?

HW: Well, that's my second point. Once you're clearer on the aims of education, then you can start making more informed decisions about the kinds of 'should' statements we discussed earlier. Rather than saying things like, 'working memory is easily overloaded, so you should do x', which runs the risk of failing to see the educational wood for the cognitive science trees, you can instead say things like, 'If you want to achieve x, then you should do y.'

AO: You two and your x's and y's. Give us an example.

HW: I can give you lots of examples. Do you remember when SLT made us take down all the classroom displays last term because they said it would increase cognitive load?

AO: Yes! That was dreadful, I couldn't believe it. And the students were furious too!

GJ: But it's a fair point, no? Surely having all that clutter around the room can only be a distraction?

HW: Perhaps, but if you were teaching a lesson in a room with displays, Grace, do you really think students would be unable to concentrate because of the posters on the walls?

GJ: If I was using my usual routines then I imagine they'd still maintain a decent level of focus.

HW: Precisely. I don't think SLT instructing us to take those posters down had anything to do with working memory. They just didn't like all those shabby old posters being up on the walls and wanted an excuse to get rid of them.

AO: How dare you call my displays shabby! I spent hours making some of those!

HW: Sorry Angela, I'm sure yours were nice.

GJ: I see your point. I can accept that in most cases those posters probably didn't have an awful lot to do with cognitive load. Can you give us another example?

HW: Sure, how about chunking?

AO: Eurgh. Another awful word. Nearly as bad as microscripting!

GJ: What's wrong with chunking?

HW: I mean, obviously there is a sound principle in there somewhere. You have to break things down to a certain extent; you can't initiate students into a discipline within a single lesson. But the obsession some teachers in this school have over chunking does drive me a bit crazy.

GJ: How so?

HW: I've seen quite a few lessons that I would describe as 'over-chunked', where the teacher is so concerned about overloading students' working memory that they only actually say about three sentences. After that, they pause and ask students to repeat those sentences back on whiteboards, before moving to exercise books and getting students to write them down again 'in full sentences'. This happens two to three times each lesson.

GJ: That just sounds like I do-we do-you do cycles to me. What's wrong with that?

AO: Apart from it being the dreariest experience you could possibly imagine?

HW: That's part of it. I often find in those lessons that the teacher looks almost as bored as the students. But it's not only that. The real problem in those lessons is that things get broken down so much that the teacher doesn't actually end up explaining anything.

GJ: What do you mean?

HW: Well, a teacher can tell students a fact, but telling them the bald fact is very different to explaining it. Explaining it means being clear about the underlying concepts. I would argue that the facts are really just the means by which we get students thinking about concepts. That's the educational wood that gets missed for the chunking trees, and chunking is a strategy that's supposedly endorsed by a body of evidence from cognitive science.

GJ: I admit that I've seen a few teachers in my department teaching like this, and the science can get a bit lost if you get too fixated on the strategies, but surely you can't deny that cognitive science has been helpful in giving us a few best bets that really work. Take the Do Now activity at the start of the lesson, which is a great opportunity for retrieval practice. Five to eight questions, the first couple with a bit of support, covering a range of topics that students have previously learned. It's also a chance to activate prior knowledge for the lesson students will be doing that day.

HW: Of course, that's pretty much our school policy. But it's not so simple, is it? Because actually, what that Do Now looks like for a high attaining class in Year 11 is very different to what it looks like for a low attaining class in Year 8. For the former, you might want more than eight questions - why not 15 or 20? - because the main purpose of this activity is retrieval and revision. You want the quiz to cover a broad range of topics, it can address some very abstract concepts, and you don't want to give the students much support. Contrast this with the Year 8 class. For them, five questions will be plenty, because the main purpose of this activity is different.

GJ: What's the purpose for the Year 8 class?

HW: I would say it's part of bringing students into your subject. Where the Year 11 students are already a long way down the road of their development, many of the Year 8 students will still experience the world in quite an intuitive and immediate way. You might want to make the questions quite easy, so they feel the success you mentioned earlier; you might want to give them extra support; you probably want to relate things to concrete contexts rather than focusing on abstractions as you do with the Year 11 class.

GJ: But all this is just good teaching. You adjust the activity depending on the class; everyone knows that. You don't need fancy sounding theories about general and specialised aims to plan a good Do Now; you just need to think about your job and constantly try to do it better.

HW: But the problem is we tend to look at our students in very narrow terms. We assume the only difference between the Year 11 students and the Year 8 students is that the older ones have lots of information stored in their long term memory whereas the younger ones don't have as much. What I'm saying is that the differences run deeper. The Year 11 students have developed a whole different outlook on life. They see themselves as learners, as people who have a responsibility to learn stuff, whereas the Year 8s are just children. They haven't started to build conceptions of themselves yet; they're just living life in a much more spontaneous way.

AO: And this is where I think both of you go wrong. What happens to those students between Year 8 and Year 11 that they lose that spontaneity and joy? What do we do to them? I think it's precisely through the kinds of endless quizzes and tests that you're talking about that we crush all the life out of them and turn them into those stressed Year 11s, desperately trying to cram all this information into their skulls without having the faintest idea why they're doing it. I get it: we have exams. I get it: employers are interested in qualifications. I get it: you think students should know things so they can take part in conversations at dinner parties. But I think you've both lost sight of the fact that in focusing on this stuff we've lost the essence of what makes life worth living. We're killing our kids, killing all the spirit and spark and energy they have when they're in primary school or younger. And all you can talk about, Henry, is how to add some scaffolds to the Do Now so they can 'feel success'. It all just seems to fall so far short of what education is all about.

GJ: You say you 'get it' about exams and employers and so on, Angela, but when I listen to you I wonder whether you really do. You admit that exams exist, right?

AO: I'll give you that one, yes.

GJ: OK, that's a promising start at least. Will you also admit that remembering more stuff makes it more likely that students will do well in their exams?

AO: Ah, there you go again. Exams, exams, exams: they seem to be the only -

GJ: No no, Angela, answer my question. Does being able to remember stuff help students when it comes to their exams?

AO: OK, Grace. Yes. Now go on, enlighten me.

GJ: Alright, so we know students will have to sit exams, and we know that remembering stuff will help them perform better on those exams, so why wouldn't we use the findings of cognitive science to help them prepare for those exams? Also, I don't see why preparing students for exams and inspiring them to study further have to be mutually exclusive. As I've said already, I think doing well on exams is what motivates students to study more, not some mythical spirit that is channelled through the teacher like they're operating some weird, pedagogical ouija board.

HW: I kind of agree with your sentiment, Grace, but I still don't think you've answered Angela's question. By talking about exams, you're really just changing the subject. As always, Angela is looking at education holistically. We all know the exams exist, and we accept that you have to do a certain amount of work to prepare students for them -

AO: Yes! Thank you, Henry. Knowledge organisers are a school wide policy. We've got them in English too. I'm not just doing shaman dances round the classroom every lesson.

GJ: Only on Fridays.

AO: Well, yes, and Thursdays.

HW: I'm on call on Thursdays; I'll have to pop in next time. Anyway, my point was going to be that Angela's argument, as I understood it, was that we want students to be the kind of people who actually *want* to learn stuff, and yet the system seems to be having the opposite effect. Is that what you meant, Angela?

AO: Exactly. Children are naturally curious and inquisitive, yet by the time they reach 16 most of them are bored and uninterested. That suggests to me that we're doing something wrong as a sector.

GJ: It's a fair point, but how do you suggest we solve it?

AO: We have to rethink both assessment and accountability. Rethink assessment so that we measure what we value rather than valuing what we measure. If we must assess students, let's look at their creativity, their originality, their ability to problem solve and think on their feet. The way exams are set up stifles these qualities and rewards those who mindlessly memorise stuff. And in terms of accountability, let's judge schools on well-being, on the number of students going into employment, on teacher retention, rather than having this ludicrous obsession with exam results. I think changing those two things would have a big impact on what teachers do in the classroom, and I think that could only have a positive impact on our students.

GJ: But we've been there before! Think back to the 90s, when I was at school, or the 50s, when you were at school, Angela.

AO: You cheeky … !

GJ: I'm joking, I'm joking, but you take my point. We used to have a system which didn't have so much rigour and accountability, and it was a system that failed a lot of children. I was OK; my parents were pushing me so I ended up doing alright out of it, but there were an awful lot of young people - I can think of friends of mine from primary school, clever kids who were never really pushed and were allowed to slip through the net. That system wasted so much talent, and we wonder now why we have a productivity crisis.

HW: I'm trying to work out where you both fit onto my general-specialised and individual-society spectrums. Angela, it seems like you want to keep things quite general and focus on the qualities of the individual person, whereas Grace, when she mentions the productivity crisis, is more interested in the measurable output of people who have been educated, which implies she's more interested in specialisation and is looking at things from a societal point of view. Have I got that right?

AO: But I'm also interested in society! If people can think for themselves then they're going to be better citizens. I also said I wanted to measure schools on their employment figures, not just on what their students can remember. And I'm open to specialisation too: I'm always very happy when my students go on to become experts in their fields or get really exciting jobs. Did I tell you one of my students recently became a published poet?

GJ: Who?

AO: Taiwo Olunloyo. She was in the same year group as Jack Stephens, Olivia Hall-Barrett, those guys.

GJ: I know, I know. It doesn't surprise me, to be honest; they were a really smart year group.

HW: Why do you think Taiwo ended up being successful?

AO: I think because she loved reading poetry, but not the kind of poetry we read in class - Seamus Heaney and Blake and all that stuff - she would read contemporary stuff, slam, rap lyrics, anything.

HW: So where did you fit into that?

AO: I don't know. I guess I modelled something to her, a sort of passion for the subject. I think she got some of that from home, too.

HW: So you don't think it's about the knowledge you equipped her with?

AO: Not at all, no. I think you could tell she was that sort of person from quite early on. I remember reading some of the stuff she used to write when she was in Year 7, and you'd just be like, "wow."

VIII

HW: It seems like we're coming back to an earlier question: what does it mean to be educated? Grace thinks it's all about knowledge, whereas Angela thinks there's something else to it, something less tangible.

GJ: What do you think?

HW: That's a very good question. I guess I think it's all about knowledge, but I would say I have a much broader conception of knowledge than you do, Grace.

GJ: What do you mean?

HW: Well, let's take Taiwo as an example. I think she's educated - educated enough to be a published poet - partly because, as Angela mentioned, she's read a lot of poetry.

GJ: This is what I was thinking. She's good at writing poetry because she's read a lot of poetry, and I expect she's had a lot of practice at writing poetry too.

HW: But I don't think it's as simple as you're making out. We talked earlier about the Year 11 high attaining students and the Year 8 lower attaining students, and we tried to work out what the difference between them was. I said that I think you have to take into account how they perceive themselves: the Year 11s see themselves as learners whereas the Year 8s probably don't have any real conceptions of themselves yet: they're still children. Taiwo is a bit further along this journey of development again. She understands herself not merely as a learner, but has now begun to take her place within a discipline. She's become even more specialised, a poet, no less.

GJ: It sounds to me like you're talking about the development of students from novices to experts. And there's a solid body of evidence to demonstrate that the difference between novices and experts is knowledge. Novices don't have much prior knowledge to draw upon, so they aren't able to synthesise existing ideas and come up with new ones, whereas experts have rich schemas from which they can make connections and easily build new knowledge. I imagine this is just as true for poets as it is for chess players or physicists.

AO: But if that was true, then how could I tell even from Year 7 that Taiwo had something, that she had that creative spark that would allow her to do the kinds of things she's doing now?

GJ: Like you said, she had a lot of support at home. I imagine her parents read books to her when she was young. Did she have siblings?

AO: Well, she had a twin, and I think she had one or two older brothers too.

GJ: So there you go, she was exposed to lots of language from a young age. I'm wary of buying into these talent stories because it makes us think some people are born with it and some people are destined to be failures. Actually, if we just focused on the things that we, as teachers, can control, then we'd limit a lot fewer students in this way. We have this amazing set of tools carved out for us by cognitive science, which can allow us to move a lot more students from the novice phase to the expert phase than we ever used to imagine. Why wouldn't we use them?

HW: But I still don't buy into your account of novices and experts. Being a novice is not an externally ascribed state or 'phase'; it's something you recognise yourself to be. I've got a friend whose partner is Finnish, so he's learning a bit of the language. I'm sure he would describe himself as a novice, and rightly so, as it's not an easy language to learn. But is he also a novice in Danish, or Urdu, or Twi? Of course not! He's not learning any of those languages, and is unlikely to start learning them any time soon. He can't even begin to qualify; he only becomes a novice when he recognises himself to be participating in that practice.

It's not like a temperature scale where you can say, 'at any temperature below $0°C$, water will be ice,' or, 'at any level of prior knowledge below x, the person must be a novice.' I think as a scientist you're looking for something measurable, but it's a whole different way of thinking that's required.

GJ: So how exactly do you suggest we get students thinking in this way? I certainly didn't see myself as some sort of neophyte scientist when I was at school. I did science A Levels because I enjoyed those subjects and was good at them. Isn't that enough?

HW: I'm not sure it is. As I said earlier, I didn't really enjoy history for most of my time at school. It just seemed to be loads of stuff to learn; I couldn't really see how any of it linked together. It was only at GCSE when I started to understand what the point of it all was. This is because I had a good teacher. She was the first person who gave me the sense that history was something happening now, in the present, not just a load of dead stuff in the past. She used to call it detective work; trying to work out how events could be pieced together into a coherent pattern. Sometimes she said it was like building a dry stone wall; taking each new stone and seeing how it would fit neatly with what's there already. And I think the greatest insight she gave me was the idea that this pattern, this wall, this historical edifice, is *our* work, not something that exists in the past, waiting to be discovered. *We*, as historians, impose the pattern; then we work out whether the evidence that's available makes sense with respect to it. That blew my mind, and once I understood what it meant to be a historian, well - I never looked back.

AO: But this is exactly what I've been talking about! History is like English; it's about meaning making. It's only when you understand how a subject relates to your own life - in the present, the here and now - that you can have any intrinsic motivation to study it. You don't learn history to learn about the past; you learn it so you can make sense of who *you* are. Likewise, you don't learn English for the sake of memorising poems; you learn how others have expressed themselves so that *you* can express yourself.

GJ: And what about science?

AO: I guess you learn about science so you can discover things and do experiments. Once you've got the hang of the scientific method then you can pretty much work everything out from there, right? It's all about knowing how to do fair tests and all that stuff.

GJ: But none of that stuff makes any sense unless you've got lots of theory behind you already! Students need to know the content before they go anywhere near an experiment, otherwise they're just playing with equipment. In our department, we always teach the theory first. When we do a practical, we model everything super slowly. This is the only way, in my experience, that the students ever get half decent results.

HW: I don't think I agree with either of you on this. What mattered was that my history teacher at GCSE gave me a sense of what the discipline was all about. I disagree with you, Angela, that it's purely about meaning making. Students are very capable of making meaning in their own lives; they don't need me as a history teacher to show them how to do it. The problem is that the meanings they make are based purely on their everyday intuitions; they assume all large scale, historical events can be understood in the same terms as the small scale, personal events that take place in the stories they consume or in their own lives. Hence they assume that history can be understood purely in terms of good and bad individuals like Churchill and Hitler, to give two obvious examples. Or they might understand national alliances in terms of friends and enemies, not appreciating that the relationships between Prussia and the Hapsburg Empire, or between Britain, France and the USSR, were a little bit more complicated than the relationships between themselves and the other students in their class.

My point is that of course we want students to make meaning from their history lessons - we don't just want it to be a list of seemingly unrelated facts - but that we want them to make *historical* meaning. We want them to understand these events in terms of historical concepts, not the everyday concepts they already have when they walk through the classroom door. If we're not helping them view the past through the lens of those historical concepts, then of course there's no point in them walking through the door in the first place. They really could just google it, as you used to say quite a lot, Angela.

AO: I've learned not to use the google argument; it's too much of a trigger for Grace!

GJ: It's just factually incorrect, Angela, but we don't need to go into that here.

AO: Honestly, the cheek of this woman. I can't cope!

GJ: Sorry, Angela. You know I love teasing you. Anyway, I agree with everything you just said Henry, so I don't understand why you said you disagree with me too.

HW: I disagreed with you on the idea that we can somehow separate the theory from the practical work. I'm not an expert on science, but in history I don't think you can make a distinction between 'the facts' on the one hand and the process by which they became facts on the other. This is how you end up with the kind of meaningless source work you were bemoaning from your own history education earlier, where you're supposed to make sense of the reliability of a source without knowing any of the context. The point is that every fact we introduce to students must be framed as part of this pattern I talked about earlier. They must see the process by which we came to know these things about the past as well as knowing the things themselves.

AO: But isn't that what I was talking about? Wasn't it Bruner who said that knowing is a process, not a product? What we need to pass on to students is the way in which facts can be discovered; that way they can find the facts out for themselves.

GJ: Bruner! You're showing your age there, Angela.

AO: Some of us did PGCEs, Grace. We actually learned something about our profession, not like in this on-the-job training you youngsters seem to think is adequate.

HW: I like it! Angela keeping things old school.

GJ: Oh God, she'll be talking about Vygotsky next.

IX

HW: To actually address Angela's argument, I see Bruner's point but I think he went too far. I think knowing has to be both process *and* product. The product on its own is meaningless, as we've been saying -

GJ: As *you've* been saying.

HW: OK, as Angela and I have been saying - but I think the process on its own is empty. You can't teach students about a concept like alliances, or democracy, or empire, without showing them lots of examples of that concept.

GJ: But that's my point! Read Engelmann: he's all about showing students loads of examples of a specific concept. That's literally what direct instruction is all about.

HW: But the danger is that Engelmann's methods lose sight of the process. You can't just say: Hapsburgs: that's an empire. 19th Century Britain: that's an empire. USSR: that's an empire. You have to show the students how the concept of empire functions within an historical argument.

GJ: What do you mean, functions?

HW: Well, I would argue that the concepts we employ within each of our disciplines function in the same way as rules. It's like we're playing chess. If you want to play chess, you have to know that bishops only move in diagonal lines. Likewise, if you want to do history, you have to know that invoking the term 'empire' commits you to understanding some historical event in a certain way. You can't simply move a bishop sideways in chess, just because you want to take the piece that's there, and similarly you can't simply call something an empire in history, just because it suits your argument. The thing that you're trying to understand actually has to fit the bill of being an empire if you're going to use that term.

GJ: But what you're talking about is definitions. You need a really clear definition of empire before you can use it in an argument. You need to know all the features that qualify it, that make it distinct from, say, a nation or a church.

This is exactly the same as what I was talking about in science, the fact that you need a solid grasp of theory before you can start doing practical work. In history, you need a solid grasp of the definitions of these words before you can start writing essays or whatever it is you guys do.

AO: But we're back to knowledge organisers! We're back to students memorising the definition of hubris then having no idea what it actually means. We only learn the meaning of a concept when we use it. You can't just get kids to memorise something like, 'an empire involves colonising smaller states, a supreme ruler, imposition of language,' or whatever, and then expect them to be able to use it properly in an argument. They need to be given the opportunity to use it for themselves so they can find out whether or not they're using it correctly.

HW: I agree. It's like with young kids. I read somewhere that the way they learn language is first by hearing words used in lots of different contexts. So I might say to my little boy, "I turned the light on," and, "it's light outside," and, "we need to put our bike lights on," and from hearing this word used a lot he begins to associate its meaning with some phenomenon that relates to his eyes. But then I turn the light on one morning and he says to me, "it's too light!" And I have to correct him and say, "it's too *bright*." And through that sort of process he learns when to use the word 'light' and when to use the word 'bright', not through the kind of abstract definitions you're talking about, Grace. It's not like I'm going to say to him, "actually, in this case the word 'light' is a noun whereas you're attempting to describe this light, and therefore need an adjective. The adjective we should use in this case is 'bright'." I just say the sentence I would actually use in this scenario and he infers how to use 'light' versus 'bright' from there.

GJ: But you're talking about a small child learning to use his first language. That's a completely different scenario to an older child learning a subject at school. Your son's brain is hardwired to remember the kind of thing you're talking about; our students have to have things explained to them in much more detail and they have to work hard to commit that stuff to memory.

HW: But isn't the reason they're having to work hard that we're thinking about our subjects in completely the wrong way? If we understood our subjects in the same way we understand languages then perhaps they'd find them a lot easier to understand?

GJ: So what does this look like in the classroom? Seriously, I'm all ears.

HW: OK, let's try to work it out. I'll have a go at science, even though it's not my subject. If we're thinking about science as a language, rather than a body of knowledge to be memorised, then we have to start by thinking about the facts we want students to remember as sentences written in the languages of the scientific disciplines. Maybe you can give me an example.

GJ: Of what?

HW: Of a fact in science, the kind of thing you want students to retrieve in a Do Now.

GJ: OK, how about, "the mitochondria are the sites of respiration within a cell."

HW: Perfect. So within this sentence, there are a few important words -

GJ: Right: mitochondria, respiration, cell.

HW: Exactly. Now I'm guessing what you want when you teach this to students is that they have a good understanding of what the mitochondria do and where they are found.

GJ: That would be nice.

HW: So to use the word 'mitochondria' meaningfully within a sentence, they're going to need to be able to use the words 'cell' and 'respiration' meaningfully too.

GJ: Definitely.

HW: Now even with my limited knowledge of science, I feel as though these two words - cell and respiration - relate to some pretty chunky concepts in science. These are the kinds of things we really need our students to understand in depth if they're going to make any sense of the subject.

GJ: Yes, for sure.

HW: So the question we need to ask ourselves is this: how are we going to get students to this sort of deep understanding of the meanings of the words 'cell' and 'respiration' required for them to understand the word 'mitochondria'? Is it just by giving them definitions and making sure they memorise them? What would be the definition of respiration?

GJ: Well, assuming we're talking about aerobic respiration, it's a chemical reaction that takes place between glucose and oxygen. It produces carbon dioxide and water and is exothermic, which means it releases energy.

HW: And here we go, you're now introducing a whole new range of concepts - glucose, oxygen, carbon dioxide, energy - that students need to understand if they're to understand this simple sentence you talked about before. And we haven't even talked about the cell yet.

GJ: They need to know about chemical reactions and conservation of mass too. What's your point?

HW: My point is that to understand one concept you have to understand this whole system of concepts. You have to understand how each of these words fits together into a network of meaning. And that's where the language analogy is helpful. Just as my son only began to understand the meaning of the word 'light' by hearing it used in lots of different contexts, in science you are going to need to use words like respiration, cells, oxygen, energy, whatever, in lots of different contexts before your students have any hope of understanding them. It's like my example of 'empire' in history, or Angela's example of 'hubris' in English. You can't understand these words until you've seen them from multiple angles.

GJ: But that's what we do already in our department. We teach them the definition first then we get them to apply that knowledge to lots of concrete examples. What you're saying is no different to what's been shown to be effective by cognitive science.

HW: How do the students do when you get them to 'apply' their knowledge?

GJ: Well, at first, awfully, but by the time they get to Year 11 they're usually pretty good.

HW: Don't you think the reason they do awfully at first is because they don't actually have a firm grasp of the concept?

GJ: What do you mean?

HW: Let's stick with the mitochondria example. How might you expect students to apply that knowledge about mitochondria in a concrete example?

GJ: One example might be explaining why sperm cells have lots of mitochondria. It's because they need lots of energy to swim up the fallopian tube and fertilise the egg. It's just one example of how those cells are specialised to carry out their function.

HW: Great - so students struggle with this when they're first asked to explain why sperm cells have all these mitochondria?

GJ: Some do, yes.

HW: I think this is because they don't really have a clear understanding of the core concepts yet. We're looking at the problem from opposite angles. You're saying: instruct them in the concept then build memory by asking them to apply that concept in lots of concrete examples. I'm saying: only through the teacher explaining how the concept applies to lots of concrete examples does the student learn how the concept functions in scientific thinking.

GJ: But isn't the outcome the same? That by the end of it, students will remember the concept?

HW: Maybe, but I'm not sure they need to memorise a definition of cell, or respiration, or energy, in order to have a good understanding of science. Is it not enough that they can apply these concepts in the kind of concrete examples you're talking about?

GJ: I guess so.

HW: This is where I get a bit frustrated with the cognitive science stuff. It's obsessed with codifying knowledge into definitions in order that the scientists have something to measure, but that's not really what knowing something is really like. Knowing something is being able to use it, almost without thinking. When teachers focus too much on the definitions, they can sometimes forget this.

GJ: But I still don't see how learning definitions is a bad thing. I think I see your point, about seeing how everything fits together. I do this via lots of retrieval questions on related topics. By having to think about things in a very tightly knit way, guided by me, students pick up this system of concepts that you're talking about. I think you can teach the kind of knowing you're talking about through memorisation of definitions; it just needs some clever, purposeful interleaving at the same time.

HW: You may well be doing this - you're a very skillful teacher - but do you think every teacher in your department is doing this clever, purposeful interleaving that you're talking about?

GJ: Probably not, to be honest.

HW: And I don't think you're even doing it in a systematic way. It's more by intuition. You just kind of *know* that it makes sense to ask a question about one thing at the same time as talking about another. That's all well and good, but if you want your team to start doing that too then don't you think you need some clearer principles upon which to make that questioning purposeful?

GJ: Perhaps.

HW: So here's my point: if you think of scientific knowledge in similar terms to learning to speak a language, then you'll use each teaching episode as an opportunity to introduce or embed a concept, rather than to apply the so-called knowledge of a definition to increasingly difficult concrete examples.

X

GJ: So are you saying we should focus less on definitions and more on building concepts?

HW: Exactly. I've seen this problem with a few of your teachers; it's almost as if they presuppose that students already understand the concept when introducing new facts or ideas. As I was saying earlier when we were talking about chunking, I would argue that the only reason to introduce those new facts is to reinforce the concept.

GJ: Go on, give me an example.

HW: I saw a lesson being taught by one of your team on the body's defences. The teacher was talking about how our skin stops the pathogens getting in; how scabs crust over to stop pathogens entering the blood; how we have those little hairs in our nose -

GJ: Cilia.

HW: Yes, those - to sort of waft away the pathogens if they're trying to get in that way.

GJ: All stuff students need to know. What was your issue with that lesson?

HW: The issue for me was that the whole lesson was being taught as if students already understood the concept of pathogens. *That's* the difficult bit for students to understand, the fact that diseases are caused by these invisible creatures floating all around us in space. We might get this; the teacher I saw certainly got it; but do the students really get it? I wasn't so sure. And the way the lesson was taught, without sufficient emphasis on that concept - pathogen - meant that all of these things the teacher was telling the students just seemed like random, disconnected items of information, rather than ideas all linked together by one thread.

GJ: I think I know what you mean. I'm doing some coaching with one of our ECTs and saw something similar to this in some Year 7 lessons on the circulatory system. I saw her teach a lesson on the heart, and she explained it beautifully: the four chambers, the blood vessels carrying blood in and out, the location of the valves, the reason one wall is thicker than the other, and so on. There was a lot there, but she drew a really clear diagram and the students were able to follow. But then I watched her teach the next lesson to the same class, which was on the blood vessels. She told them how the arteries have thick walls, how the veins have thin walls and valves, how the capillaries are very tiny. I was watching the students and they seemed overwhelmed. I was trying to figure out what she could have done differently.

HW: It's what we were talking about earlier, isn't it? That to understand any one of these concepts you need to understand the whole system of concepts. I imagine there's one or two underlying ideas that link everything in that system together?

GJ: It basically all boils down to respiration and circulation.

HW: So this is precisely my point. Everything you teach them in that unit, whether it's the thickness of the walls in the heart or of the different blood vessels, needs to be related back to those underlying concepts.

GJ: I always come back to the diagram showing the double circulatory system when I teach that unit. If they understand that, everything else makes sense.

HW: That's exactly what I mean! And this was the problem with the body defences lesson: the teacher was telling students lots of facts, but I don't think he was explicit enough about how these facts were related to one another in terms of the concept of pathogens. As a result, I'm not sure that everything he was telling the students really made sense to them. It just came across as a stream of arbitrary facts they were somehow expected to remember.

GJ: So how could that teacher have made the concept clearer?

HW: This is where things are going to get controversial. I was thinking about this after watching that lesson, and I felt that what was missing was the *history* of the concept.

GJ: Oh, here we go.

HW: Hear me out, hear me out! You remember I said that in history, we are imposing a pattern upon the events of the past in order to try and understand what happened. Well, I think the same thing is happening in science. We are imposing structures on what we observe in the natural world to help us understand it better. Of course, humans must have always known that scabs go crusty and that we have hairs in our nose. The point of biology is to understand *why* we have these things. I'm sure people made all sorts of suggestions about this in the past - maybe we have hairs in our nose to keep our nose warm, just like we have hair on other parts of our bodies - but it was only after we became convinced that diseases are spread by pathogens that the 'body defences' idea became the standard reason given. This is the kind of pattern the scientist imposes: the concept of 'pathogens' is a rule that governs how we must think about phenomena like scabs and hairy noses.

GJ: This is interesting, although I'm not sure where the history of the concept comes into it.

HW: Well, I think you need to show your students the significance of the concept, and I think the best way to do this is by guiding them through its historical development. It was Pasteur who effectively proved the existence of pathogens, wasn't it?

GJ: Yes. He did the experiment with the swan-necked flask.

HW: Exactly, and I assume there was some other theory doing the rounds at that point which Pasteur put to bed?

GJ: Now you're testing me. I think there was this idea that diseases and mould and things like that spontaneously generated. Pasteur had the idea that there must be something getting in from the air in both cases, whereas the other main argument was that disease was a malfunction in the organism or tissue itself.

HW: That's super interesting, right? And surely to understand the concept of the pathogen and how it relates to disease, you have to understand why it gives a better explanation than this other conception of disease. It's a bit like my son misusing the word 'light' when he should have used 'bright'. We have to test out students' thinking, tease out these ideas they already have about the world. It seems to me that teaching students about Pasteur would have been a good way to develop the sort of understanding we're looking for. You don't get this sort of comparison -

GJ: 'Cognitive conflict', you mean?

HW: Precisely! You don't get the cognitive conflict if you just skip straight to the correct answer. I think that's what it is that frustrates me with the cognitive science stuff. It implies that you can just go straight to the answer and that students will magically remember it. It doesn't seem to take into account any of the concept building that's required.

GJ: Again, I think you make some good points, but I still don't see how this should be a core part of the curriculum. We're science teachers, not history teachers. We do cover some of this hinterland stuff, but the main thing I want my students to take away is the stuff the teacher you saw was focusing on, the core knowledge. I worry about the split attention effect when it comes to all this extra stuff. It may all be very interesting and engaging, but doesn't it stop

106

students thinking about what we actually want them to think about?

HW: But I'm not advocating teaching students about Pasteur just because it's a bit of fun and engaging. I agree that's very dangerous. I once saw someone else in your team teaching a lesson about vaccines. They showed a cartoon about how Edward Jenner came up with the idea of the vaccine to treat - what was the disease he treated?

GJ: Cowpox. The word 'vaccine' comes from the Latin for cow.

HW: There you go! I watched that video yet now I can't remember that, which seems like a fairly fundamental fact.

GJ: What do you remember?

HW: Well, that's just it. What I remember is that there was this maid in the video, and she'd been drawn - how should I put this? - with an extremely curvy figure. Literally every single boy in the room was sniggering. I remember thinking, they're going to remember nothing about vaccines from this. They're just going to remember that funny video with the busty maid. It had been put in there as a bit of interesting historical background, but it ended up taking away from what the teacher wanted the students to learn about.

GJ: That's my point. Why not just tell them the facts?

HW: But I think you should teach about Jenner. I think it's really important: it's another way of reinforcing the idea that diseases are caused by pathogens. What that teacher should have done is draw students' attention to the process Jenner was following. First, he noticed that the maids didn't seem to get cowpox. He used the concept of diseases being caused by pathogens to come up with the idea that they must have been exposed to the pathogen and somehow developed immunity. From this, he worked out that if you could give someone a very tiny amount of the pathogen - enough to expose them, but not enough to kill them - then they too might become immune. And then he tried it out -

GJ: Yes! On the eight year old boy. You wouldn't get that past an ethics committee these days.

HW: Absolutely not, especially the bit later on when gave the boy a whopping great dose to see whether he got ill or not.

AO: Goodness me! What happened?

GJ: He didn't get ill. The vaccine had worked.

HW: Exactly. So here we have the scientific process in a nutshell. Jenner used the concept of the pathogen to work out what he'd expect to happen if he gave a small amount of the cowpox pathogen to the boy. He then tried it out to see whether what happened agreed with his predictions. When it did, he could continue with confidence that the concept of pathogens was the correct one.

XI

GJ: So you think we should teach all this about Jenner, and Pasteur, and every other scientific discovery? I don't know how we'd get through the content if we were to do all that.

HW: Perhaps you won't teach students about every discovery, but if you want them to build an understanding of these concepts then I think you have to have some history in there somewhere. Sorry, Angela, you haven't managed to get a word in edgeways for the last five minutes. What do you think?

AO: I'm not sure I followed all of what you were saying - I'm not a scientist! - but I thought it was interesting. I don't think the same principles can be applied in my subject though. There's no accepted history of English literature - well, maybe there is if you're Michael Gove, but I'm not too interested in what he has to say. And I just don't think you can reduce English down to concepts in the way you guys are talking about in history and science. Every student makes their own meaning.

HW: I'm not sure I agree with you. Surely you need a decent working knowledge of the bible before you study Milton? Surely you have to understand a little bit about Pope before you can understand just how revolutionary Wordsworth and Coleridge were? Surely you need to know something about life in Victorian England before you attempt to read Dickens?

AO: But there you go again, reeling off all those dead, white men! It might be acceptable to do this in science - my guess is that the history of science you guys are talking about is almost exclusively European - but you certainly can't do it in English. If we want students to learn to express themselves, then they need to read texts they can relate to. Why not study contemporary rap lyrics? Aren't these just as powerful forms of expression as what was written in the 1600s?

HW: I think this takes us back to the general aims of education. As a society, we want our students to leave school with certain shared meanings with which they can understand one another. Hence there *are* concepts that can be found in some of the classic texts - good and evil, authenticity, the unconscious - that we want every student, regardless of background, to be familiar with. Likewise, as individuals, these concepts can help students make sense of their lives in ways they would not be able to if they didn't attend school.

My fear with trying to relate texts to students' everyday lives is that we risk failing to equip them with the *literary* concepts that allow them to go beyond their current worldview. It's through these concepts - these rules that govern how those participating in that discipline think about themselves and the world - that we carry out the transformation you alluded to earlier.

AO: But even if I grant you the existence of concepts in English for the sake of argument, although I remain sceptical, I still don't think your argument about history stands up. Why do students have to have this same old diet of Shakespeare, Milton, Wordsworth, Dickens, whoever? Of course, I can see why from the nation building point of view - that would be the argument of Gove or E.D. Hirsch - but my argument is that the purpose of schooling is the opposite to that. It's about freeing students' minds, not indoctrinating them with some nationalist myth.

HW: I take your point, but I feel as though you're neglecting an important aspect of schooling. Initiating someone into a culture or tradition is not a bad thing. In fact, I would argue that it's an absolutely essential aspect of education. It's the only way we can find genuine meaning in life, insofar as it gives us the means with which we can relate our experiences to those of others.

We can come back to the language metaphor. We'd never have any literature - whether contemporary or classical - if we didn't have a language, and learning a language means submitting oneself to an authoritative structure. You could call it nation building or indoctrination, but that kind of misses the point. Without participating in a language, you could scarcely be called a person. I think something similar could be said about participating in knowledge. Take poetry as an example: don't you think you need some sense of where the practice of poetry has got to today before you commit pen to paper yourself? Otherwise, you're destined to either repeat the kinds of things that have been written already or write meaningless babble that no one except yourself can understand.

AO: Another classic case of liberals patronising those who aren't like them! You're not a person if you don't speak a language? You can't write poetry unless you've studied 'the canon'? Tell that to someone with SEN. Tell that to indigenous people who have been displaced by white settlers. Tell that to a working class kid on the wrong side of your so-called 'vocabulary gap'. You know what they'll tell you? They'll tell you where you can shove your opinions.

GJ: But I don't see where your argument leads us, Angela. I'm not sure I follow all Henry's waffling about general and specialised and initiation, but I do know that schooling is surely a waste of time if students leave without learning the meanings of new words, about new concepts and facts, about the knowledge that's been discovered across the range of subjects.

AO: No! I want them to leave with an attitude, with an orientation, with a set of qualities. You just care about what they *have* when they leave school: all that stuff you want to fill their heads with. I'm more interested in who they *are*.

HW: But this is my point! What I'm saying is that who they are depends on the practices and disciplines they participate in. This is as true for the marginalised groups of people you mentioned just now as it is for the poet or physics professor. The cultures they are a part of - the family, the local community, whoever - have their own 'common sense' knowledge, their own systems of concepts, their own histories. Students arrive at school already part of these practices; what I'm saying is that we need to introduce them to other practices too.

AO: Why? What's wrong with the practices they are part of already?

HW: There's nothing wrong with them, per se; it's just that the disciplinary communities we're talking about have made some incredible discoveries about the world, society, and the human condition. Firstly, I think we owe it to our students to pass these on to them. Secondly, from a practical point of view, there's no way our students will ever be able to understand those who grew up outside their local community if we don't introduce them to these broader ways of making sense of the world.

GJ: Exactly what I've been saying all along!

HW: Well, kind of, but where I go further than you, Grace, is to say that we must give students a sense of the process of discovery as well as getting them to remember what has been discovered.

GJ: This sounds alarmingly like 'discovery learning'. Is that what you're advocating?

HW: No, absolutely not. The idea of discovery learning, it always seemed to me, was that students would just stumble across the answers to some of the biggest problems humanity has grappled with, which seems optimistic to put it mildly.

Now I think about it, the word 'discovery' is a bit misleading. It implies that this stuff is out there in the world waiting to be found. I guess what I'm talking about is the pattern again. What tends to be called a discovery is really just a pattern imposed upon the world by a great thinker to help them make sense of what they're studying. We must show students these patterns, as you have been arguing, but we must also show students how the patterns imposed by scientists, for example, are different to the patterns imposed by historians or in literature. And we must help them appreciate the rules inherent in each discipline that give knowledge a status beyond, "Einstein said this," or "Steinbeck said that." The concepts of the discipline reflect the collective rules that have been accepted by a whole community of practice; that's the sense in which they can be understood as objective knowledge rather than subjective assertion.

GJ: I still don't see why this stuff matters as much as you're banging on about. The fundamental point is this: we decide what we want our students to learn, then we find the best way of helping them to learn it. Isn't that all there is to it?

HW: But this assumes that the status of all knowledge is fixed and that, in terms of the curriculum, all we need to think about is sequencing.

GJ: Which is pretty much the case in science. The same could be said for maths, too.

HW: I disagree! Perhaps if you're a specialist already, you can take all these scientific facts as givens, but if you're an eleven year old child then they must come across as deeply problematic. Take an example I saw you teaching, recently, Grace, about heat transfer. You were talking about opening the fridge door -

GJ: Yes, and how energy is transferred from you to the fridge, not the other way round. The classic misconception there is that there is a thing called 'coldness' being transferred from the fridge towards your hand.

AO: Is that not what's happening?

GJ: No, what's happening is that your body temperature is a lot higher than the temperature of the air in the fridge.

Consequently, because energy is generally transferred from the hotter object to the cooler object, your body transfers heat to the fridge. What you experience as a blast of cold air is actually a rapid loss of heat from your body as it heats the air in the fridge.

HW: Which is all well and good, but that's not how most people make sense of what's happening in that situation. A child certainly isn't going to think about it in those terms; the account you're giving is deeply counter-intuitive. Hence you can tell a Year 7 student all you like that there is no such thing as coldness, but you're going to have to do a lot more than that to make them really believe it. How to get them to *believe* what we're telling them; that's the fundamental question we need to answer.

GJ: Isn't this just a denial of what we know to be true? Aren't you implying that everyone can have their own opinion and that there's no such thing as objective truth?

HW: Not at all. Anyone who knows how the kinds of concepts you're talking about developed will be pretty confident that they give a much better account of the phenomena than our everyday intuitions. The problem is that students *don't* know how these concepts developed. What they're confronted with is a teacher who tells them that everything they thought about the world is wrong, that they need to forget all these intuitive concepts that have been perfectly adequate to them up until now and adopt a whole new range of concepts instead.

AO: This is what I was saying before! It always seems to end up boiling down to: I'm the teacher, believe what I say, even when the story keeps changing, like with atoms. The students who are willing to trust the teacher get labelled as 'high ability'. These tend to be the middle class ones with parents who have told them they have to listen to what the teacher says. The students who don't trust the teacher, who aren't willing to let go of the understandings that have helped them make sense of the world up to that point - they get labelled as 'low ability'. And who are these students?

GJ: Working class and minorities, I know, Angela. You've told us already.

AO: But you see my point? Ultimately, it's a question of power. And my challenge to you is, why is it only you who gets to decide what students should learn? And who says your knowledge is the best knowledge?

GJ: If you take that view, I just don't see how you can teach anything. How can you be a teacher?

XII

HW: I think we're getting close to some pretty fundamental questions, which hopefully will help us address my original question about knowledge. It seems to me that a lot of teachers in our school have adopted the kind of attitude to knowledge Grace has been talking about. They're taking the knowledge of their disciplines as a given, which reduces curriculum thinking to a process of sequencing. But the curriculum is not a barcode. There's way more to it than sequencing.

GJ: So what do you think is involved in designing a curriculum?

HW: If we're going to take Angela's arguments seriously, which I think we should, then we're going to have to totally rethink the knowledge we stipulate in the curriculum. And I don't just mean questions around 'the what' - what we put into the curriculum and how we sequence it - I mean questioning what 'the what' is in the first place.

GJ: You're losing me, Henry.

HW: I guess we need to understand how curriculum knowledge differs from disciplinary knowledge. What you're talking about as knowledge, Grace, is an abstraction from someone already steeped within a discipline. It looks at various experts and says, all of these people would be able to tell me this, this and this. It's the codification of expertise into information. Your approach is to say, 'OK, I know that experts all think this, and this, and this. My job is organise this information into the correct sequence and find the best methods for committing it to students' long term memory.'

This might work, if students were already steeped in the discipline and just needed to remember stuff. Perhaps it's no coincidence that a lot of the educational methods influenced by cognitive science - retrieval practice, spaced practice, interleaving, and so on - came from university lecturers and professors supporting their undergraduate students in their revision. The problem we have here in a secondary school is that the vast majority of our students *aren't* already steeped in the disciplines. They don't yet see themselves as part of our disciplinary communities: they're novices in the way I was talking about, not just in terms of the information stored in their long term memory. Simply telling them how a disciplinary expert thinks isn't going to change who they are. That's the problem we have to grapple with.

What we need is an understanding of knowledge that is always in close relation to the way students think about the world at that point in their education. Curriculum knowledge is always relative to the everyday or intuitive knowledge students bring with them into the classroom. It's not just an abstraction from an expert; that's too far removed from their current worldview. It's an idea or experience that challenges their current worldview and helps them make sense of the world in terms of our disciplinary concepts.

GJ: This goes back to what you were talking about before, right, about cognitive conflict and all that stuff?

HW: Exactly. We need a curriculum that is pedagogic, not static. It's not just, 'tell them the facts then get them to remember them'. It's, 'help them see the world in terms of disciplinary concepts, then show them how these concepts give better explanations of phenomena or events than their everyday intuitions.'

The point is that the concepts - the rules that govern how we think - must come first. The facts are necessary - they're the only way students have access to the concepts, in the same way that sentences are the only way we can actually use words - but it's only after we've got students thinking in terms of the concepts that we can package the facts up and do retrieval. Just like chess is moving pieces by following rules, knowledge is thinking about the world in terms of concepts. That has to be the basis of our curriculum thinking.

GJ: So you're saying we shouldn't be separating questions around curriculum and pedagogy? Are you saying they're really just one and the same thing?

HW: I'm not sure. I guess I have a sense that these various aspects of schooling aren't quite as distinct as we tend to imagine. Obviously, we have our Assistant Principal for behaviour, our Assistant Principal for teaching and learning, our Assistant Principal for curriculum, and so on, yet in practice these all seem to be inextricably linked. We all know that students are more likely to misbehave for a teacher whose pedagogy isn't quite on point. Likewise, a teacher whose knowledge of the curriculum is excellent can be a bit looser around routines and behaviour and still get excellent results.

AO: Yet again, this is what I've been saying! We need to let teachers teach! Too often, we crush their autonomy for the sake of consistency, when if we would just let them be themselves in the classroom then their students would perform better.

GJ: Come on, Angela. You don't really believe that do you? Look at the schools who really drill down hard on consistency of routines. Their outcomes are amazing, especially for the lowest prior attainers. The kind of Dead Poets Society model you're talking about might work for some students - typically the top set kids - but you end up with different kids getting a different deal depending on which teacher happens to be standing in front of them. I just don't see how that's fair.

HW: What kind of routines are you talking about?

GJ: The kind of things we're doing in the science department. We've been thinking really hard about open questions vs closed questions. If a teacher is asking a closed question, they have to be getting a whole class response, just as Rosenshine talks about. This may be through whiteboards, it may be through call and response, it may be through fingers up - whatever.

AO: Why does it have to be a whole class response?

GJ: So we don't embed misconceptions. It drives me crazy when I see teachers doing cold call for closed questions. If the first student answers incorrectly, there's a risk that all the other students will remember that and not the correct answer. Doing it whole-class avoids this problem as well as giving the teacher an instant snapshot of what the students are thinking. I don't see why you wouldn't do a whole class response for that sort of question.

AO: I don't see why you would ask that sort of question in the first place. The sort of question you're talking about doesn't really get students thinking; they either know the answer or they don't. I'm much more interested in asking the kinds of questions that spark a debate. I suppose you'd call those open questions?

GJ: I would, and I think there's a role for those, although you shouldn't overlook the importance of closed questions, Angela. Again, read Rosenshine: he talks about how master teachers ask a high frequency of closed questions. It's all about retrieval: the more often you try to retrieve information from memory, the more likely you are to remember it next time.

AO: You and your Rosenshine, Grace! I've heard all this before, but I'm still not convinced. Can't you do all this stuff in the Do Now at the beginning of the lesson, so that you can get onto the more interesting stuff later on?

GJ: You can, but asking lots of questions also creates a super positive culture. Students like being challenged to think; they like it when the teacher demands that they pay attention. I've been thinking about cold calling a lot recently; I've always done it with no hands up but I've heard people saying that asking students to put their hands up is a really good way of generating a buzz in the room. It's something I want to try out in our department, although maybe not until next term. At the moment we're still working on the mechanics of a turn and talk. It's taking a long time to get that nailed. You're looking puzzled, Henry. What's up?

HW: I'm just interested in what you're saying. I guess this is what I meant by considering curriculum and pedagogy as completely separate things. When I listen to you speaking about teaching and learning, I worry that you're doing so in a way that's overly specialised. This way of thinking runs the risk of becoming so fixated on micro details of pedagogy - whether to pose a question to an individual student or the whole class; whether to have hands up or no hands up; whether to use whiteboards or do a turn and talk - that you can lose sight of the bigger picture altogether.

AO: Precisely what I've been saying. All this talk about Rosenshine means we're missing the point of what education is actually all about.

HW: Well, not quite Angela. I don't think talking about Rosenshine is a bad thing. I think we *have* become better teachers since we started implementing those sorts of policies at a whole school level. The problem is that we've become overspecialised, like I said.

GJ: What do you mean?

HW: I guess there's a danger that if your team become experts in the mechanics of a turn and talk then they may lose sight of the fact that a turn and talk is just a means to an end, i.e. getting students thinking about the answer to a question the teacher has asked. Part of a teacher's job is finding the best way to get students thinking, of course, but another part is choosing the right questions to ask in the first place.

GJ: I see what you mean - like the teacher you observed teaching mole calculations but not really teaching the students about moles.

HW: Exactly. The teacher there was executing the pedagogical strategies pretty much perfectly, yet the concepts weren't coming through. This is what happens when you overspecialise: your practice fragments and you start to compartmentalise things. You end up losing that balance between thinking about pedagogy and thinking about concepts. I suppose this is the flipside of what I was saying about the curriculum having to be pedagogic: pedagogy must always be driven by the curriculum too.

GJ: But that's why we have our CPD sessions on pedagogical content knowledge. They're an opportunity to think about teaching and learning strategies in relation to a particular topic or concept. I think they bring together the things you're talking about.

HW: Which is great, but I know not every department in the school is running those sessions.

AO: And you still haven't addressed my point, Grace, about how you bring the passion, the spark, the energy through. You talked about culture just now, and said that hands up questioning instead of no hands up questioning might be the key to creating a positive culture. I think that's nonsense! The culture is set by the teacher themselves, not the strategies they're employing. If students are inspired by their teacher, then there'll be a positive culture. If they find the teacher boring, there won't be. It's that simple.

GJ: So how can we ever make teachers better? Does every teacher have to be this insanely charismatic, deeply knowledgeable, incredibly hard working hero that you're talking about? We're in the midst of a retention crisis, Angela! The teachers you're talking about just don't exist, at least not in the numbers we need to make sure every child gets a fair deal. I would much rather focus on the things we can control, like the strategies teachers use to maximise how hard students are thinking in lessons, than throw our hands up in the air and despair that not every teacher is as perfect as you are.

AO: Was that a compliment, Grace? Are you OK?

GJ: It was, and yes, I am, Angela. I hear you, I really do. Deep in my heart, I think I probably feel the same way as you, but a year and a half of being head of department has rid me of a few illusions. I'd be delighted if every teacher was inspiring in the way you're talking about, but try recruiting an inspiring science specialist. There aren't many out there. It's not to say I don't have a good team: they're amazing. They're smart, they're willing, they genuinely want the best for the students. But if I just leave it up to them to work their magic - well, you know how that's going to go.

AO: I take your point. It's tricky.

XIII

HW: Well, this must be a first. You guys have actually managed to see something from each other's point of view.

AO: Miracles do happen, Henry!

GJ: I don't know what came over me. Angela must be doing her shaman thing again.

HW: In all seriousness, I think we're making progress. We're coming back to what we've been talking about all along.

GJ: Which is … ?

HW: Knowledge. Trying to understand knowledge in a way that makes learning meaningful for students. This means thinking about the curriculum without losing sight of pedagogy, and thinking about pedagogy in a way that doesn't forget the curriculum.

GJ: It's a nice phrase, Henry, but I'm not sure I actually know what you're talking about.

HW: Let me try to spell it out a bit more clearly. You guys have disagreed on a number of things so far. As I said earlier, the main thing seems to be in terms of parts and the whole. Grace wants to break everything down into parts, whereas Angela always wants to start with the whole. Whether it's breaking down a text or starting with the broader meaning; thinking about pedagogy in granular terms or bundling it up within the personality of the teacher; managing behaviour via adherence to codified rules or via relationships; all these are basically manifestations of two fundamentally different starting positions. And I think your starting positions are just reflections of your subjects. Grace is a scientist, hence she wants to break everything down and discover the mechanics of it, whereas Angela is a poet, hence she wants to maintain the unity of human experience.

AO: As one of your beloved dead, white men said, "we murder to dissect".

GJ: Who said that?

HW: Wordsworth, wasn't it?

AO: Very good, Mr Welwyn. Michael Gove would be proud.

GJ: I haven't read any poetry since I did my English GCSE, so I wouldn't know. Anyway, what's your position, Henry? Whose side are you on?

HW: Well, that's it. I'm a historian so I don't want to take either side. I want to understand why you guys can't agree with one another and try to find a way forward.

GJ: Good luck with that one.

HW: Thank you, I'll need it! Let's look at where we are now. At the moment, the theories and techniques Grace has been talking about are having a big impact on whole school policies. We're doing lots of retrieval practice, lots of checking for understanding, everyone's talking about ratio. In many ways, I think this is good. Like I said before, I think the drilling down and focusing on our teaching and learning practice has - unsurprisingly, I suppose - made us better practitioners.

GJ: I sense a 'but' coming.

HW: You sense correctly. The problem is that, in directing all our attention towards these cognitive science-inspired techniques, we've become overspecialised. This has led to two issues. Firstly, in becoming expert pedagogues, we've forgotten about the curriculum. We've neglected our roles as embodiments of our disciplines. This is what I was talking about in the examples I gave earlier: the teaching practice in all those cases was on point, but the disciplinary concepts were getting lost.

GJ: And your solution to this was to introduce the history of the discipline into our teaching.

HW: Exactly. Since we started shifting our whole school approaches towards the TLAC, Rosenshine, Willingham-type stuff you've been referring to, teachers haven't been asked to actually read up on their subjects. I think that's one thing we urgently need to address: how can we bring curriculum thinking and pedagogical thinking back together in order to develop subject-specific teaching strategies? I know you do a bit of this through your department CPD, but it's not something that's happening across the board.

AO: What was the other issue?

HW: The point you keep coming back to, Angela, that we've lost sight of the broader, ethical role we have as teachers. I agree with you that we can't reduce good teaching down to a set of strategies. I feel as though there's a moral, almost spiritual, aspect to education which gets lost in the kinds of theories Grace has been advocating.

GJ: So how do we solve this?

HW: Well, again starting from my position as a historian, I think that if teachers had a better understanding of the history of their disciplines then they'd have a clearer idea of what makes studying their subjects worthwhile.

AO: 'Worthwhile'. Not a word you hear used much in our whole school CPD sessions these days.

HW: Not much at all, but I think it's key to bringing back together these different elements that have become fragmented through specialisation, without losing sight of the gains we have made as a consequence of focusing more closely on our teaching and learning.

GJ: In what way?

HW: At the moment, it feels as though we've become so specialised that students don't have any connection with the ways of thinking characteristic of our disciplines. We need to show them how these ways of thinking fit into a broader conception of a good life. In other words, how does studying literature, science, history, art, music, Spanish, whatever, make you a better person?

AO: A better person? I can hear alarm bells ringing!

HW: I'm sure you can, Angela, but if we want to make education meaningful for our students then we're going to have to grapple with some difficult questions like this one. I just don't think you can be value-neutral on these concepts, and pretend that there aren't better or worse ways of making sense of the world. You *do* know a lot about Shakespeare, and Wordsworth, and Dickens, alongside all those other authors that someone like Taiwo has grown up on. You're part of this tradition, whether you like it or not. In fact, I would say that's the only reason you're able to critique it. It's only because you know how all those dead, white male authors attempted to understand the world that you are aware of the limitations of their worldview.

AO: But aren't you just parroting Grace now, and E.D. Hirsch, and all those other liberals who want everyone to be able to read the New York Times and spout off at dinner parties?

HW: No, because that argument takes everything within a discipline as given. As you said earlier, it presents all this stuff as the end of the conversation, whereas I'm arguing that we must help our students *join* the conversation. If we're going to achieve this, then they need a pretty decent overview of where the conversation has got to already. This means teachers having a thorough knowledge of the history of their discipline, as I've been saying, and also being expert pedagogues in order that their students have a chance of understanding - and remembering - what they're talking about.

What Hirsch didn't talk about, and Grace hasn't said much about this either, is the kind of open-ended questions, tasks and projects that I think you'd like to see more of across the school. These look forwards rather than backwards, hence making our teaching both the end *and* the beginning of the conversation at the same time. Knowledge is only useful if we use it, if it changes the way our students interact with the world. This is what I meant by a pedagogic curriculum. Instead of thinking about the curriculum as a list of facts that just needs to be sequenced, we have to start thinking about it in terms of concepts. How can we curate the experiences students have in a way that gets them thinking in terms of those concepts? Once you shift to that mentality, questions around sequencing become far less important.

GJ: So you're saying I tend to see teaching as the end of the conversation whereas Angela tends to see it as the beginning, but that in actual fact it needs to be both.

HW: Yes, that's exactly what I'm saying. You put it much more succinctly than I could.

XIV

GJ: This is all very interesting, but I'm not sure I see how it's going to affect my classroom practice.

HW: OK, so let me ask you a question, Grace. Who are you when you're teaching your subject?

GJ: What do you mean? I'm Grace.

HW: Well, if you take my way of thinking seriously, then you're not Grace, because Grace is a person who participates in a whole range of communities and practices. When you stand in front of your students teaching them science, you're only representing one community: the disciplinary community of biology, chemistry or physics.

GJ: Perhaps I should get myself a badge.

HW: Perhaps, but what I'm saying goes deeper than that. My way of thinking places the subject at the centre of the room, not the teacher themselves. If, when you're in your classroom, you see yourself as an embodiment of your subject, then there's no distinction to be made between those lessons where you're telling kids facts and those lessons where you're modelling procedures. In every science lesson, you're there to model a way of thinking, a set of disciplinary rules that bind together anyone who can be thought of as a scientist.

GJ: I see what you mean, although I'm not sure it's quite so clear cut. We often lump all scientists together under one bracket when in actual fact the way biologists think about the world is very different to the way physicists and chemists think about the world. Biologists tend to focus on larger systems, whereas physicists and chemists want to reduce everything down to the smallest units possible. There's a school of thought in biology that wants to do this too. It's a live question.

HW: That's amazing! So the science curriculum is still contested, at least to a certain extent. That implies there really is more to building a science curriculum than sequencing: what you're saying suggests there are some big, unresolved questions that you can get your students thinking about.

GJ: It's true, and there are various debates around the nature of reality going on in quantum physics too.

AO: I love quantum physics! It sounds so cool.

HW: Were you taught it at school?

AO: God no! All I got taught was a load of dry facts that I can't even remember now. I've just read bits and bobs about it as an adult and it sounds fascinating. I wish I understood more about it.

HW: So there you go: another great example of the kind of thing we ought to teach to our students as part of a general education. Angela doesn't need to be an expert in quantum physics -

GJ: Yes, I seem to remember the maths involved in quantum physics being horrendous.

HW: Exactly - but surely our education system owes her at least some sort of working knowledge of roughly where the discipline has got up to and a sense of the questions that remain unanswered?

GJ: I suppose it does.

HW: So that's another way in which thinking about the history of your discipline can change your classroom practice: it influences the decisions you make about what you actually teach.

GJ: But you're going to have to be pretty careful about introducing some of those difficult topics, aren't you? I'm not going to start teaching my Year 7s about quantum physics any time soon.

HW: That's where you have to think about the curriculum pedagogically. What experiences could you offer students to give them a glimpse of some of these unresolved questions? How could you show them that to study science is to participate in a conversation that's still ongoing?

GJ: Good questions. I'll have to think about them.

HW: I don't have any answers but I'd love to keep discussing. Anyway, I want to get back to what I was saying about who you are in the classroom. You're not just Grace any more: you're an embodiment of your subject. When you introduce a fact to your students, you're not just skipping straight to the end and saying: "mitochondria are the sites of respiration in a cell," and expecting kids to remember it. You're modelling the thinking process that led to that fact being established as a fact.

GJ: How am I supposed to do that?

HW: Let me give you an example from history. If I'm teaching Angela's favourite topic, the Tudors, to my students, then by the end of it I'll want them to know that Henry VIII broke from the Catholic Church and established the Church of England. I could just tell students that bald fact, but, if we're going along with the broader conception of knowledge I've been arguing for, they're not really going to *know* it, even if they can remember it and retrieve it in quizzes at the beginning of the lesson.

If I want them to really know it, I'm going to need my students to understand something about the relationship between church and state. This means they're also going to need a decent knowledge of kingship and the idea of divine right, of the Catholic Church and the role of the pope, and of the worldview of ordinary people in medieval England. There's a lot there, so I'm going to have to make sure I address those ideas in lessons that come before my unit on the Tudors even begins.

GJ: So you need to make sure students have the requisite prior knowledge before you introduce this new knowledge. That's no different to anything I've been saying.

HW: But your notion of 'prior knowledge' seems thin. The point is that when you introduce those ideas you're doing more than just telling students stuff. I mentioned church and state because I watched one of my team do this brilliantly recently. She was telling students a story about Thomas Becket: how he'd been a good mate of Henry II, how Henry had installed him as Archbishop of Canterbury so he could sideline the Pope, how Becket changed his tune and began to get in Henry's way, how Henry had Becket executed, how we know about Becket's execution because of a particularly grisly description written by a monk, how the public turned against Henry because Becket had been so popular, how the Pope fast-tracked Becket to sainthood as a one-in-the-eye for Henry, and finally how Henry paid his penance by having himself flogged while wearing a hair shirt.

AO: That sounds brilliant! The students must have loved it.

HW: They did, and I think what made it amazing was the way in which the teacher spun them a yarn. She kept pausing, asking seemingly trivial questions - "What do you think Henry did next? How do you think the Pope felt about that? What must have been going through Henry's mind when he heard the news?" - that actually conveyed the essence of what it means to be a historian. She wasn't telling the story in a dry, 'this happened, then this happened, then this happened' sort of fashion. She was telling it in a way that recreated the whole world at that time, or at least enough of the world for students to get a feel for it. She got inside the characters' heads; she gave students a sense of what it was each character had to weigh up; she drew their attention to the pressures each one faced and the ambitions they were trying to satisfy.

Of course, you could turn everything she told them that day into a retrieval quiz and call it 'prior knowledge', but that would be to overlook all the other work she was doing in that lesson to bring the subject to life. *That's* what I'm talking about when I say we must be embodiments of our subjects. It's all those little things we do, often without even thinking about them, that mark us out as representatives of our disciplines.

AO: But isn't this just the same as what I've been trying to argue? The reason she's a brilliant teacher is that she has that passion, that inspiration. She could be teaching any subject and she'd do a brilliant job. What's important is that she brings learning alive for her students -

GJ: She lights their fires.

AO: She does! Isn't that what being a good teacher is all about?

HW: Of course, I see where you're coming from, but I disagree that she could be teaching any subject. What makes her special is the extent to which she's a historian. All those little questions she was throwing in, all those seemingly insignificant details, these are things only someone steeped in the discipline could do. If you got her to read a poem with students, or model one of those chemistry calculations we were talking about earlier, well - I think she'd do a pretty mediocre job. She wouldn't be *able* to perform in the way she did in that lesson on Thomas Becket, just as you guys wouldn't be able to teach that lesson anywhere near as well as she did.

GJ: Yes, yes, I see where you're coming from now. I always think about this stuff when I'm modelling calculations: all that metacognition, narrating the thought process stuff we did in CPD a few months back. I'd never thought about it when teaching straight up facts, though. I'm trying to think what it might look like in science.

HW: I guess science is less about stories.

GJ: Definitely. If we started telling stories to students then we'd be losing the science altogether I think. The whole point of science is that it doesn't fit together nicely into one coherent narrative.

HW: I suppose I would start with the point I made earlier, that the history of science is going to be a useful starting point in terms of finding the major concepts. So, if we go back to the mitochondria, what were the big breakthroughs that helped us understand what was going on?

GJ: Harvey discovering circulation. Lavoisier working out that respiration was basically the same as combustion, once he'd got a clear picture of what oxygen was. van Leeuwenhoek and Hooke coming up with the idea of cells.

HW: Right, so the power of these concepts is that they explain an awful lot of stuff. And my understanding of science is that the explanations tend to take the form of, 'if this happens, then this happens, then this happens,' and so on.

GJ: Pretty much, yes.

HW: And that's very different to history, of course, which has much more complicated and messy causal relations.

AO: And English, which doesn't really think about causation in that way at all!

HW: We need to come back to English later.

GJ: It's almost as if what the teacher needs to do in science is say, "OK, Harvey put forward this idea that blood circulates around the body, picking up stuff and dropping stuff off. If Harvey's idea was true, then we'd expect stuff to be picked up from the lungs, because we know already from everyday experience that the heart rate and breathing rate are somehow linked."

HW: Exactly! And we might ask questions like, 'what would you expect to happen if … ?' These are the sorts of questions scientists ask. They're similar to the questions we ask in history, but where in history we're trying to understand the decisions and actions of the people involved, in science you guys are trying to understand things in terms of impersonal mechanisms and processes. Have I got that right?

GJ: Well, not quite, but it'll do for now. But yes, I like your question: 'what would you expect to happen?' That's the kind of question we could ask later in that unit. I'm thinking of the lessons we do around the effect of smoking on exercise: "If you smoke, then what would you expect to happen when you exercise?"

HW: And you could just tell students that, right? You could say, smokers can't exercise as effectively because …

GJ: Because they can't get as much oxygen into the bloodstream and therefore can't respire as quickly. But yes, rather than just telling them these facts we can model the thought process that gets them there. I like this: I'm keen to try it out.

HW: Please do, and let me know how it goes. Let's talk about English, Angela. Who are you when you're in the classroom?

AO: Well, my answer would always have been 'me', but I suppose you want me to think about it differently to that.

HW: Yes. I guess I'm asking whether you're a poet, a novelist, a literary critic, a journalist, an academic scholar. Who are you? Now I think about it, it's quite complicated, isn't it?

AO: It is, and I think this is often overlooked by SLT. They think all subjects are the same, and we're really not. Who am I when I'm in the classroom? I guess I'm all of them. That's what makes it difficult.

HW: It's one to consider. Because the way you read a poem with students, for example, is going to be different if you're modelling the thinking of a poet compared to the thinking of a literary critic. And you have to consider whether you even want to model something so specialised. Do you want to show them how a literary critic thinks or just someone who has a decent general education?

AO: I would probably say the latter, but I'd have to think about it more carefully.

XV

GJ: I like what you're saying about modelling, Henry. I still don't think there's anything wrong with calling stuff students have learned already 'prior knowledge', but I take your point that we have to do more than tell students the facts if we want them to understand stuff.

I'm still a bit concerned, though. I want my CPD to be super targeted and actionable, and telling my team that they have to be representatives of their disciplines or embodiments of their subjects is not going to give them something they can take into the classroom the next day. How else is thinking historically about our disciplines going to help an ECT who's got a bottom set Year 9 to teach on a Thursday afternoon?

HW: It's a good question. I think one thing you guys could learn from historians relates to the way we model historical thinking and writing. If I'm reading a text in history, I want to direct students' attention to how the author uses language to convey a certain historical meaning.

There are words in each sentence which we relate to what we call first order or substantive concepts. These are the kind of concepts that students need to have seen across a variety of contexts if they're going to understand them: alliance, institution, modernity, and so on. The bulk of our teaching is really just a means to getting these concepts across, as I've been saying. The facts we teach our students are just a means of conveying the concepts, a point which is often overlooked.

GJ: This relates back to what you were saying about the pathogens lesson earlier, right?

HW: Exactly. So that's the vocabulary of a sentence we're reading or constructing, but there's also the grammar to consider.

AO: Oh God, I sense you're about to start talking about fronted adverbials and subordinate clauses.

HW: Not really. I'm aware of those approaches -

GJ: You mean The Writing Revolution stuff?

HW: Yes. I think there's a role for that sort of teaching somewhere, at some point, but in history I want to make sure that everything comes back to *historical* concepts, not just general grammatical rules. We call these second order or disciplinary concepts.

GJ: So you're saying each subject has its own grammar?

HW: Potentially, yes. As I said earlier, the way we think about causation in history is very different to the way you guys think about it in science. In science, there's pretty much just one mode of causation: if this happens, then that happens. It's mechanistic: the pattern we're imposing on the world is based on the presupposition that everything can be understood in terms of processes. In history, it's a lot messier. There's no one clear conception of causation. We just have to use words like 'triggered' or 'facilitated'.

GJ: Can you give examples?

HW: Sure, so we might say something like, "The First World War was triggered by the assassination of Archduke Franz Ferdinand." The word 'triggered' does a lot of work here: it conveys how there were all these factors that, in hindsight of course, were building up and building up, and that it took just one tiny event - you could think of it as a domino - to kick off what turned into four years of mass bloodshed. This is different to something like the Holocaust. Students often think of the Holocaust in terms of a very simple perpetrator-victim model: Hitler was the baddie; he killed all the Jews.

AO: That's pretty much how I got taught it.

HW: I'm sure; it's not something that's taught well at all in English schools. What we need to teach students is that there are lots of factors which were necessary but not sufficient as 'causes'. I put that word in inverted commas because it's not really clear cut, as I've been saying.

GJ: What were those factors?

HW: Well, in very simple terms, antisemitism, which itself has a history that goes back way beyond 20th Century Germany. Secondly, Hitler himself and his position as a consequence of World War 2. Finally, you have to frame the whole thing in terms of the Industrial Revolution, mechanisation, 19th Century science, and so on. Only with that much broader context can you understand how so many people could be involved in something so terrible.

GJ: So you can't just put it down to, "Hitler was evil, therefore the Holocaust happened."

HW: Absolutely not. My point was that in this case we might say something like, "The Holocaust was *facilitated* by scientific, economic, and technological developments in the 19th Century." That's a very different notion of causation to that involved in Franz Ferdinand being shot, and it's different again to the kind of causation you guys are dealing with in science.

GJ: And you teach this stuff to students? It sounds pretty ambitious to me.

HW: We try. The point is that when we read historical texts or model historical writing, our aim is to draw students' attention to the historical concepts - first or second order - rather than just thinking about it in terms of how to pass an exam.

GJ: That's interesting. I observed one of my team teaching Year 11 recently. He was modelling how to answer an exam question, but it didn't really seem like modelling to me. He was just telling them what the marking points were. It was an 'explain' question on how mosquitoes transmit malaria. He said to the students something like, "First, I'm going to write that mosquitoes carry the pathogen and are therefore called vectors. Next, I'm going to write that mosquitoes bite human beings. Finally, I'm going to write that the pathogen enters the bloodstream and the person becomes infected." I watched him and thought, you haven't modelled anything here. There was no thought process, nothing they would ever be able to use to answer another question. It was literally just, here's how you would get three marks on this particular question.

HW: We have the same problem in history: here's what you need to do to get nine marks on this exam question. It's the tunnel again, the underground train: it gets them to the marks but they've no idea how they got there. It loses the disciplinary element entirely.

AO: But surely you need some structures like that? When I'm teaching students how to answer Q5 on Paper 2 of the Language exam, I give them the structure and they follow it. That's how they get the marks.

GJ: I thought you were all about inspiration, Angela! That sounds even drearier than one of my lessons!

AO: I accept that we have to do what we have to do for the sake of exams. If I was education secretary, I'd do away with the whole system, but while the exams are there I'm going to train my students on how to pass them.

HW: I get it; the history GCSE doesn't always test historical thinking either. There are recipes for quite a few of the questions that students just need to practise in order to get good grades. But I think the bulk of what we do in the classroom *should* be more discipline-focused, something more ambitious and expansive. In science, I guess it would hinge on that word 'explain'.

AO: You do a lot around command words already, don't you?

GJ: A little bit. Whenever an 'explain' question comes up, I tell my students that explaining is all about giving reasons. How does this work? Why does this happen?

AO: I saw one of your team give students a nice model for these questions, actually. He called it SHARK: S for Stop! Read it. H for Highlight keywords. A for Are there instructions? R for Read again and think about your answer. K for Keywords: write down the keywords you'll use. He had a nice little icon of a shark to help students remember the method. Isn't that the kind of thing the other teacher could have modelled so students at least had some sort of process to follow?

HW: But every step in SHARK is completely generic. There's nothing in there that couldn't be applied in a written question in history, geography or DT. I would argue that the science team should be modelling how to explain things *scientifically*, and that requires a lot more thought.

GJ: Go on.

HW: This is where the history of the discipline comes in again. We talked before about how science develops when someone comes up with a powerful model that seems to explain lots of things. These explanations take the form, "if blood circulates around the body, then it must pick up oxygen at the lungs." That 'if … then …' grammatical structure is characteristic of scientific reasoning.

GJ: And maths, I suppose.

HW: True. Either way, I think it's those sorts of grammatical structures that you need to model to your students. It's through understanding those that they begin to understand the rules which govern how concepts are related in your subject.

GJ: I think this feeds into the way we draw our diagrams too. I often get frustrated that the diagrams my teachers draw are little more than illustrations. They don't always seem to serve much of a purpose. Perhaps this is a way of making them more meaningful.

AO: I can't believe it, Henry. Grace is talking about meaning! What have you done to her?

GJ: But I really did always want science to be meaningful to my students. It always just felt like an either/or. Either you made it meaningful through discovery learning and interdisciplinary projects, or you just got on with teaching them the facts. The former was fun and 'engaging' but students never learned anything. The latter seemed a bit less fun at first but I always found I got better engagement because students actually knew what I was talking about. What I like about what Henry has been saying is that you can kind of do both.

AO: This is very exciting! Shall we do a play about atoms?

GJ: No way will you ever find me doing a play. That wouldn't be a science lesson: it would be drama. But when it comes to atoms - the history of atomic models for example - Henry's got me thinking about how I might lay out the diagrams I draw and how this might support my students' writing.

XVI

HW: I'm going to have to go soon.

AO: Me too. My kids are going to be wondering where I am!

HW: I've really enjoyed chatting to you both. It's been fascinating to hear about what's going on in your departments.

GJ: Definitely. We should do it more often.

HW: I don't know whether we've got any further in understanding how to do our jobs better. Have we?

AO: Does it matter? As you said before, Henry: it's not about the destination, it's about the journey!

HW: Did I say that?

GJ: You said some stuff about going to Oxford Circus to do some shopping. Anyway, I think it has helped. I definitely want to look a little closer into the historical aspect you were talking about, Henry. I thought that was interesting. It made a lot more sense to me than all that stuff you were saying about general and specialised.

HW: I don't think I've cleared that stuff up in my own head either. As I said earlier, I'm not sure we can ever clear it up. I think part of being a teacher is having to juggle these competing ends of education.

AO: Don't forget the ends I've been talking about: students being inspired to learn more and think for themselves.

HW: But I think that's just part of a general education. That's what education used to be about in medieval times. You had this idea of *liberalitas*, which basically meant being a decent sort of chap -

AO: It would be a chap, wouldn't it.

HW: Of course - so the aim of education in those days was to help members of the nobility turn out to be kind-hearted and generous citizens. Hence students studied the liberal arts - or the *artes liberales* if you want to sound fancy and

Latin - which gave them a grounding in all the major branches of human thought. Once they were done with that, they could leave school behind and go away and study for themselves.

GJ: It doesn't sound like they were doing interdisciplinary projects and group work.

HW: I suspect not, but the goal was pretty much the same as the one Angela has been arguing for. The difference was that education was only available to a very select few, and those who didn't study hard just dropped out. No one was forcing them to stay in school.

AO: Sounds brutal!

HW: Well, it kind of worked because at that time everyone had a place and was generally happy with it. If you were a nobleman you might wish to study rhetoric or mathematics, but if you were a peasant you wouldn't even think of such things. We have a very different mindset now.

GJ: So what's your point?

HW: Well, there's an interesting period of history, around the end of the 18th Century and the beginning of the 19th Century, when the aims of education changed. This reflected changes that were going on in the wider world too. Previously, every educated person had been a generalist. You were expected to know a little bit about everything and be able to relate your learning in one area to your learning in another. This is why you had such amazing concept makers, people like Copernicus, Galileo and Newton who could bring together their knowledge of mechanics and their knowledge of astronomy and show that actually these were all part of a unified system.

GJ: They called scientists 'natural philosophers' in those days, didn't they?

HW: Exactly, because 'science' as a set of disciplines hadn't become fully specialised and distinct by that point. Hence you had thinkers like Descartes and Pascal, who came up with fundamental concepts in mathematics and physics, but also wrote classics of philosophy and theology. You'd never find people like that nowadays, because to come up with anything new you have to become so specialised.

AO: So how did education change?

HW: This is where it gets interesting. In England, education - and I'm talking primarily about universities here - began to change quite a lot around this time. Science was progressing, the industrial revolution was taking place, labour was becoming ever-more divided as factories and the like sprang up, and education began to shift to reflect these developments. To serve the needs of the economy and empire, it was deemed necessary to train students in the most powerful methods of subjects like maths and, later, science. Hence, education became more specialised and that general notion of *liberalitas*, of everything being tied together by one unifying thread, began to get lost.

In Scotland, things were different. There, they stuck to the old principles for a lot longer. Their mathematics professors were less interested in teaching students the most powerful methods and more interested in discussing the premises upon which mathematical knowledge was based. Students didn't specialise until much later on. There were English professors who came up to Edinburgh in the early 1800s and were appalled at how little maths the students seemed to know. Instead of learning the algebra needed to crunch through the kinds of problems students tackled at Cambridge, students attended large seminars discussing arcane matters relating to Euclidean geometry - What is the nature of a line? Is it ever possible to have a point in space? - that sort of thing.

GJ: The English being appalled by the Scottish education system. Sounds familiar!

HW: Doesn't it?! This stuff goes back a lot longer than Alex Salmond and Nicola Sturgeon.

Anyway, another interesting difference between the English and Scottish education systems was access. In England, education was the preserve of the elite, those students who would go on to become part of the ruling class. First, they went to the old grammar schools or public schools, then to Oxford or Cambridge. If you weren't wealthy and part of the Church of England, your options for a university education were severely limited. In Scotland, on the other hand, courses were pretty much open to anyone, regardless of background. Where in England the aim was to train an elite band of students to go away and run part of the East India Company, in Scotland, there was this ideal of an educated public, a society full of people who had a solid understanding of all the branches of knowledge and how they related to one another.

AO: Sounds incredible!

GJ: And exactly what I would love to see. Was this ever any more than an ideal, though?

HW: I'm not sure it was. Certainly there have been books written that make out as if Scotland did achieve these broad, general aims. It's hard to tell how much of that is myth-making, however.

GJ: Either way, it's something we can aspire towards.

HW: It certainly is.

AO: But we're still a million miles from that in this country! Grace loves to bang on about social justice and how everyone has an entitlement to powerful knowledge or core knowledge or whatever the latest buzzword is, but it doesn't change the fact that, for most of our students, school is still this awful, punitive thing that's done to them rather than something they take part in willingly themselves.

Science is a great example. I'm afraid to say it, Grace, but I think the way I was taught science, which I don't think is all that different to how your department teaches science, benefits very few students. It's great for those students who, for whatever reason - usually linked to their parents' education or income - get it. Most students, though, and I count myself in this category, don't get it. They're just trained in these methods which seem completely abstract and pointless. My challenge to you is this: how are you going to move away from this 19th Century English model to something closer to what Henry was describing as having been in place in Scotland?

GJ: I appreciate your challenge, Angela. I think I've always thought of the science curriculum as either a training to go on and study further or as something that will help students to make sense of their everyday lives. Hence I gave you those examples at the beginning of this conversation about wiring a plug and putting screen wash in my car. But I think what he's talking about is different to this.

HW: It is. I guess the point of a general education is to give students a sense of how scientific knowledge is constructed, which goes hand in hand with the question of what it means to think scientifically. What's important is that when a big political decision needs to be made that is somehow related to science -

AO: Covid would be an obvious example.

HW: Yes, that's a great example - what's important is that our students can appreciate the various ways of thinking about something like covid and come to a sound judgement about what's best.

AO: So not, "trust the science."

HW: Not at all! That was a clear sign that someone like Boris Johnson only had a very limited understanding of science.

GJ: That or he assumed that the general public didn't really understand science.

HW: That too. Anyway, in an ideal world, surely we want our students to be able to think, 'I can see the scientific arguments for locking everything down immediately' -

GJ: 'If we lock down the country, then the r number reduces. If the r number reduces, then there is less pressure on the NHS ...'

HW: I can hear you modelling it to your students now, Grace! So we want them to be able to see those arguments, but we also want them to be able to weigh those up against the social, political, economic arguments. What will be the impact on the population's physical and mental health if we lock down? Will the government get support for a lockdown policy? How are we going to afford a lockdown if it causes the whole economy to grind to a halt?

AO: It was never just a scientific question, was it.

HW: No, and anyone with a decent general education would have been able to recognise that.

AO: But what about that moral dimension? What about that spiritual, ethical aspect of education? Have you addressed that?

HW: I think that's part and parcel of what I'm advocating. Go back to the concept of *liberalitas*. It's based on the idea that having an education in the *artes liberales* makes you a kind-hearted and generous person. Or read Confucian philosophy from Ancient China. Did you know that in those texts the word for heart and mind is the same? The heart was thought to be the thinking organ as well as the centre of one's moral being. There was no distinction between knowledge and goodness in their thinking: to be knowledgeable was to be a good person. They weren't endlessly trying to divide and specialise as we do in our culture; things were much more unified.

AO: Do you really think studying the academic disciplines makes you a better person?

HW: Yes, because by studying the major disciplines, you learn to take perspectives outside of your own. You learn to overcome the falsehoods and narratives spun to you by authority, or your ego and its sense of wish-fulfilment, and begin to see things as they really are.

GJ: I'm still not sure I buy your argument. Most artists or scientists or historians are not kind-hearted and generous. They're selfish, overambitious, proud -

HW: But that's because they're overly specialised! They've devoted so much of their life to pursuing their chosen field that they've forgotten the basic things that make you a decent person. They're unable to balance these competing priorities they have to contend with in life.

GJ: So you're saying that we shouldn't encourage anyone to specialise?

HW: Not at all. As I said earlier, the tension between general and specialised education, both at an individual and societal level, is something we have to work with. Specialisation is a good thing in many ways. By devoting all their energies to very specific problems, the scientists of today have achieved things that the natural philosophers of the 16th and 17th Centuries could only dream of. I don't think the problem is specialisation per se; it's that we've lost sight of the general aspect of schooling. Perhaps this is related to the decline in religion and the rise of ideologies in the 20th Century, I don't know.

The upshot is that everyone is becoming increasingly specialised and we're beginning to fragment. This is happening at an individual level - look at the burnout epidemic and the mental health crisis amongst teenagers - as well as at a societal level, where political discourse has become increasingly polarised because people have become so detached from one another's worldviews. These are big problems, and it's our role as educators to try to solve them.

XVII

AO: I'm just waiting for Grace to ask how any of this is relevant to classroom practice.

GJ: You beat me to it!

HW: Well, firstly, it frames our curriculum choices. Choosing what we teach is not as simple as selection and sequencing. We have to be clear about the history of our discipline if we're going to give students a general education that's worthy of the name.

GJ: What does that look like?

HW: It looks like students being fluent in the vocabulary of the discipline as well as its distinctive grammar, so they have a decent appreciation of its major achievements and are clear on how the knowledge it has generated is distinct from the knowledge of other disciplines.

AO: Don't forget them being able to *use* whatever we teach them so that they can think for themselves.

HW: That too. We need to think about the curriculum in pedagogic terms so that whatever we decide to do in the classroom takes their current worldview as the starting point, not the worldview of someone already steeped in the discipline.

The flipside of this is reimagining pedagogy in much more subject-specific terms. At the moment, we imagine pedagogy as some generic thing that works just as well in PE as it does in RE. Actually, if we think about education in general-specialised terms, we realise that each subject has its own distinctive voice in the conversation. It's our role as teachers to help our students speak in that voice - the vocabulary and grammar I referred to just now - by showing them how to use language in a subject-specific way.

GJ: Through the word choices, and the modelling, and the layout of the diagrams …

HW: Precisely. So that stuff all helps them specialise, but it also needs to be framed in a whole school curriculum policy which shows that these different ways of thinking are all just that: different ways of thinking. We need to remind both staff and students that schools exist to help you think in different ways, more powerful ways than the 'common sense' ways of thinking students are likely to be exposed to if they only interact with their families and local communities.

GJ: So it's about the subject-specific pedagogy, but also how that's framed at a whole school level.

HW: Yes, and again you've put it much more succinctly than me. Finally, if we take the general-specialised distinction seriously, then we can address the critiques Angela has been putting forward about education being a somewhat meaningless exercise for many of our students.

AO: Typically those 'low ability' students from working class or ethnic minority backgrounds.

HW: Exactly. If we, as teachers, understand our role not only as instructing students to become part of our disciplines, but also in learning to view the world from multiple perspectives outside their own, then I think education becomes a deeply meaningful endeavour. It's what enables us to understand the perspectives of others more clearly. I think that's an educational ambition we should have for *all* students, regardless of their circumstances or background.

GJ: All this sounds lovely, but again it's very high level and I'm not sure it's what my team and I need to be worrying about right now. As long as kids need to know stuff for their exams, surely our focus has to be on finding the best bets for securing them the very highest outcomes.

HW: I get it, but I think you should be careful not to neglect the questions we've been discussing. What is knowledge and what does it mean to be knowledgeable? You're still thinking about knowing stuff in terms of little items of information stored in long term memory. I'm saying it's something more profound than that, that to know is to recognise oneself to be part of a practice, to consciously follow the rules accepted by the disciplinary community, to have the power to interact with the world in ways that you couldn't otherwise. If we only focus on exams, then there's a danger we lose sight of all this.

GJ: But that's exactly what I'm doing for my students! I model things then get them to practise precisely because I want them to be able to do things they couldn't do otherwise. The quality of this practice depends a lot on their prior knowledge, so extensive retrieval practice is necessary to get them to the point at which they can become the kind of person you're talking about.

AO: But what's missing is that self-recognition. Henry's saying that the student has to begin to see themselves as part of the discipline if we want to call what they have 'knowledge'.

HW: And it's not just about them seeing themselves as part of the discipline: others have to recognise them as being part of that discipline too. That's where I think you and I differ, Angela. You give too much weight to the individual student. If they think they're a poet, they're a poet, and no one has the right to claim otherwise.

I'm saying something slightly different. I'm saying that every discipline has its history, and through that history certain concepts have evolved. These concepts act in the same way the rules do in a game, a game being something that also has a history, with rules that have developed over time. At any given moment, the rules of a game are widely recognised by everyone who plays the game. If you don't know the rules of a game - let's continue with the example of chess - then you might think you're playing chess, but actually you're just moving bits of ivory around on a wooden board. Likewise, if you aren't in possession of disciplinary concepts, then you might think you're doing poetry, chemistry, history, whatever, but you're not going to be recognised as being knowledgeable by anyone who really is part of that discipline, because the way you're going to think isn't constrained by those disciplinary concepts.

GJ: I think I'm beginning to see what you mean. All those examples you gave earlier, about moles and pathogens and mitochondria: you're saying that students can only be described as being knowledgeable if they have a firm grasp of these concepts?

HW: Yes. It's only through being clear about the role of these concepts that they'll be able to give reasons for what they're thinking, rather than just blindly memorising things. To take that example about sperm cells again, we don't just want students to remember that sperm cells have lots of mitochondria, we want them to be able to give reasons why sperm cells *must* have lots of mitochondria, in terms of all the other concepts that are related to these ideas. That's what knowledge is: being able to give reasons for what you think and evaluate the reasons given by others.

GJ: But aren't you just doing exactly what you've accused me of, trying to reduce knowledge and education down to something understandable in terms of your subject? You're telling me we all have to teach the history of our disciplines; I'm saying we need to consider the science of learning. Aren't these just two different ways of understanding knowledge? And if that's the case, then who's to say that your way of understanding is any better than mine? Isn't it quite helpful sometimes to think of knowledge in terms of items of information that students need to memorise? It certainly seems to help students get good outcomes.

HW: Of course that can be a useful way to think about it; all I've been saying is that it isn't the only way. You've said it yourself, Grace, that you can be a bit bossy -

AO: 'A bit': there's an understatement!

GJ: Come on, Angela, I thought we were starting to understand one another!

HW: My point is that I agree with you: there *are* various ways of understanding what it is that's going on in classrooms. I accept that the scientific approach is helpful when it comes to exams, because science is based on observation and measurement and exams are really just a form of measurement. It makes total sense that if your focus is on that form of measurement, then the science of learning is going to equip you with some very useful tools.

What frustrates me is that certain members of SLT like to bang on about cognitive science as if that's the *only* way of understanding what we do. I happen to think the historical way of understanding knowledge is helpful too. It brings out the importance of concepts, which are crucial in teaching our subjects in both a general and a specialised way. I also think it captures the ethical dimension of being a teacher that Angela has kept reminding us of, which is essential if we're going to give students a general education as well as a bank of specialised techniques.

What matters is that we all have different perspectives and place our emphasis on different things. When it comes to securing amazing outcomes, I want to hear from Grace about what the scientific evidence suggests works best. And when it comes to creating an incredible classroom culture, I want to observe Angela and get a feel for what it is she does that makes her students tick.

The point is that we don't need to constantly argue with one another. We've been having a conversation, not a debate. There doesn't need to be an overall victor; we don't always need to conform to one person's idea of what good teaching looks like. But equally, we all have to be ready to listen and to learn from one another. We're doing lots of interesting things within our subject areas: it would be a shame if these stayed within siloes rather than being shared across the school. I guess it comes back to the general-specialised thing again -

GJ: Of course it does!

HW: Of course! We have to be specialised in our subject areas and without losing sight of our broader, more general goals. This means pursuing our practice in an incredibly single-minded way, but never forgetting that we must, at the same time, be open-minded and ready to adjust what we do in the light of new arguments and ideas. It's hard, but if we keep talking, and keep listening, then we'll keep improving what we do.

GJ: I like it. I'm still not 100% convinced but I've certainly enjoyed the conversation.

AO: Me too. Thanks guys!

HW: Thanks guys. I look forward to chatting again soon.

Printed in Great Britain
by Amazon

32057373R10109